THE REFERENCE SHELF   VOLUME 36 NUMBER 2

THE PEACE CORPS

EDITED BY PAULINE MADOW

THE H. W. WILSON COMPANY
NEW YORK   1964

THE REFERENCE SHELF

The books in this series reprint articles, excerpts from books, and addresses on current issues, social trends, and other aspects of American life, and occasional surveys of foreign countries. There are six separately bound numbers in each volume, all of which are generally published in the same calendar year. One number is a collection of recent speeches on a variety of subjects; each of the remaining numbers is devoted to a single subject and gives background information and discussion from varying points of view, followed by a comprehensive bibliography.

Subscribers to the current volume receive the books as issued. The subscription rate is $12 ($15 foreign) for a volume of six numbers. The price of single numbers is $3 each.

PREFACE

An objective of the United States Government in the post-World War II period has been to help war-devastated and underdeveloped nations attain freedom from want—one of the four freedoms for which the United States and its Allies fought in the second global war. Since the end of that conflict the United States has undertaken several programs—the Marshall Plan, Point Four, Alliance for Progress, Food for Peace—directed largely at realizing this aim. This volume is concerned with one of these ventures: the Peace Corps.

The basic premise of the Peace Corps program is that the disparity in standards of living among nations is one of the underlying conditions that lead to war. Thus, to help developing nations improve their material circumstances is to advance the cause of peace. For at the same time that material improvement is made, a new and deeper awareness and understanding of the common aspirations and beliefs of mankind, regardless of nationality, can be achieved by placing people of different countries together and surmounting the barriers of language, customs, economic activities. The Peace Corps attack on war is twofold: economic and psychological.

It required little argument to convince the American people that peace serves the best interest of all, for the tragic consequences of continued hot and cold warfare were only too well understood. To prove, however, that the Peace Corps would serve the national purpose and help emerging nations required a demonstration of the corps' effectiveness. When it was first established, there were some derisive and skeptical criticisms. At home it was called "Kennedy's Kiddie Korps," a "haven for draft dodgers," another "giveaway" program. Abroad it was viewed in some quarters as intervention by a foreign power and a manifestation of imperialism.

3

Responding to the late President John F. Kennedy's call in 1961, several thousand Peace Corps volunteers—many of them young men and women fresh from college—went overseas to provide trained manpower desperately needed by developing nations. By working with underprivileged people in these areas, they began not only to alter the popular misconception of the average American, but also to gain new insights themselves into foreign lands and peoples. Other nations are now emulating the Peace Corps idea by establishing units of their own. In three short years the Peace Corps has proved its worth.

Although the Peace Corps is associated with Kennedy in the public mind, President Lyndon B. Johnson has adopted his predecessor's position on the corps. On December 14, 1963 Johnson signed a bill authorizing enlargement of the agency, and one month later he requested an increase in its budget to $115 million for the fiscal year 1965. As Vice President he helped formulate its policies while serving as chairman of the National Advisory Council for the Peace Corps. He was chairman of the International Conference on Middle Level Manpower, sponsored by the Peace Corps in October 1962, and he headed the United States delegation to that conference.

Included in the following pages are descriptions and evaluations of the Peace Corps, its origins, its operations, and its accomplishments, set forth by Government officials, observers of world affairs, and others.

The editor is indebted to the authors and publishers for granting permission to reprint material in this compilation, and is especially grateful to the Public Information Division of the Peace Corps for supplying various data and documents.

PAULINE MADOW

March 1964

CONTENTS

PREFACE 3

I. ORIGINS AND OBJECTIVES

Editor's Introduction 9

Henry S. Reuss. A Point Four Youth Corps ....
.... Commonweal 10

John F. Kennedy. An Alternative to Military Service ......
.... New York Times 17

John F. Kennedy. A Permanent Peace Corps 20

William James. The Moral Equivalent of War 25

H. G. Wells. World Order in Being 29

Samuel P. Hayes. Promise and Problems of a Peace Corps .. 32

II. RECRUITING, TRAINING, AND ORGANIZATION

Editor's Introduction 40

Charles E. Wingenbach. Training in Action—Project Tanganyika 40

Operations of the Peace Corps 46

Jean Ellickson. Librarian in the Peace Corps ....
.... Wilson Library Bulletin 53

R. Sargent Shriver, Jr. The First Year Was Tough ....
.... Vital Speeches of the Day 57

III. Accomplishments

Editor's Introduction 68

Fulton Freeman. Community Development in Colombia ... 69

Pioneers .... New Yorker 81

Milan J. Kubic. Señor Ron .... Newsweek 86

Peace Corps Couple Typify New Trend ....
.... Chemical and Engineering News 88

Margaret Michelle McEvoy. "You Just Plunge In" ....
.... Peace Corps Volunteer 91

John F. Kennedy. Enlarging the Peace Corps ....
.... Department of State Bulletin 96

R. Sargent Shriver, Jr. Peace Corps Successes 99

IV. Extending the Peace Corps Idea

Editor's Introduction 105

John F. Kennedy. Domestic Youth Services 106

Gertrude Samuels. A Peace Corps for Our Own Bleak Areas
.... New York Times Magazine 110

Helen B. Shaffer. Opposition to a Domestic Corps 116

Harlan Cleveland. A United Nations Peace Corps ....
.... Department of State Bulletin 117

David Rockefeller. Businessmen Organized for Peace 120

V. Evaluation

Editor's Introduction 123

Benjamin DeMott. Objective: Local Democratic Action . . . .
. . . . Harper's Magazine 124

Thomas W. Ottenad. The Peace Corps Wins Its Way . . . . .
. . . . Progressive 131

Unsentimental Journey . . . . Economist 137

David Barnett. Volunteers Resent "Hero" Role . . . .
. . . . Peace Corps Volunteer 140

R. Sargent Shriver, Jr. Some Questions and Answers 146

Roy H. Hoopes, Jr. Challenge and Response 149

R. Sargent Shriver, Jr. The Peace Corps' Strength . . . .
. . . . Foreign Affairs 158

BIBLIOGRAPHY 164

I. ORIGINS AND OBJECTIVES

EDITOR'S INTRODUCTION

Perhaps no other program, domestic or foreign, reflects so well the spirit and philosophy of Kennedy's presidency as does the Peace Corps—its experimentation, its altruism, its accent on youth, and its roots in American thought. In a bold stroke President Kennedy created a temporary Peace Corps by executive order in March 1961, without benefit of congressional approval or specific appropriation. Congress met the President's challenge by establishing a permanent Peace Corps in September of the same year, soon after the first corpsmen went overseas.

In his conception of a peace army, Kennedy was inspired by the idea of redirecting to peaceful pursuits the dedication, sacrifice, selflessness, and physical fitness engendered by war. The basic idea was expressed by William James at the turn of the century in his essay "The Moral Equivalent of War." Later H. G. Wells, influenced by James's views, prophetically outlined plans for replacing marching soldiers by dedicated scientists and teachers in his utopian world-state; these plans could have been blueprints for the Peace Corps. Originally, in a 1960 speech, John F. Kennedy had recommended that young men serve in the Peace Corps as an alternative to peacetime military service. Such a proposal was embodied in Senator Hubert H. Humphrey's Peace Corps bill of 1960 and was an important topic of the study provided for by a legislative act of 1960 sponsored by Representative Henry S. Reuss, Democrat of Wisconsin, and the late Senator Richard Neuberger, Democrat of Oregon.

Although under the Peace Corps Act of 1961 young men who serve in the corps are not exempt from military obligations, they can obtain deferment from their local draft boards for Peace Corps duty (regarded by Selective Service as in the national interest) and are not disqualified from further deferment upon leaving the corps. When volunteers return home, they are often beyond the age limits established by the Selective Service System. Therefore, in practice, duty in the Peace Corps is for many individuals an alternative to military service.

The idea of the Peace Corps also developed from the experience of the many thousands of American religious missionaries who worked among foreign peoples. It was further influenced by the examples of the prewar Civilian Conservation Corps and of private organizations, such as the American Friends Service Committee and Operation Crossroads Africa, which sponsor overseas service programs.

This section explores the purposes of the Peace Corps as expressed by leaders of the executive and legislative branches of the Government, traces its origins in writings of William James and H. G. Wells, and presents a summary of its background by Samuel P. Hayes.

A POINT FOUR YOUTH CORPS [1]

When I was in Cambodia studying our foreign aid program, I was struck by the oft-observed contrast between the militarism-encased-in-concrete approach and the Johnny-Appleseed approach. We have a large-scale program of military assistance to the Cambodians, but so far the only time that the American M-1 rifles and tanks were used was when the Cambodian government was liquidating other Cambodians suspected of being too friendly with neighboring Thailand and Vietnam. We have a large program of "economic aid," of which the crowning jewel is a superb American-built highway stretching from the capital, Phnom Penh, to the sea. But, while gratifying to the country's rulers, since it makes them independent of their neighbors, the superhighway's largest meaning for most Cambodian peasants lies in the use of its shoulder as a trail for their water buffalo.

[1] From article by Representative Henry S. Reuss (Democrat, Wisconsin). Mr. Reuss served in Europe as Deputy General Counsel for the Marshall Plan. Commonweal. 72: 146-8. My. 6, '60. Reprinted by permission. (The term "Point Four" is derived from President Harry S. Truman's Inaugural Address, delivered on January 20, 1949, in which he recommended a four-point program to ensure peace and freedom; Point Four was a program of technical assistance to developing nations which has since been a part of all United States foreign aid programs.—Ed.)

Recently, when I told the historian Arnold Toynbee about the Cambodian road, he observed that many mature civilizations have a passion for building straight and beautiful highways from the center of civilization to its outer edge—whereupon the barbarians come down the highway and wipe out the civilization!

In truth, I do not believe that the Cambodian highway is necessarily a hallmark of the decline of the West. But I would feel a lot more confident if our emphasis were more on some of the good things I saw us doing in Cambodia, such as the team of four American schoolteachers—a Negro from Chicago, an Italian girl from Brooklyn, among others—who were going through the jungles helping the villagers to set up their first elementary schools, something the French in a century of colonial rule had neglected to do. This was a brave new world, and the Cambodians loved it.

Uneasiness about the flavor of our foreign aid program led me recently to introduce a bill, cosponsored by the late Senator Richard Neuberger [Democrat of Oregon], to study setting up a Point Four Youth Corps of young Americans willing to serve in technical assistance missions, in far-off places and at a soldier's pay. Obviously, and understandably, a large part of the public interest in the Point Four Youth Corps idea has been generated because it offers a possible alternative to military service under the draft. This element is, however, only one of many compelling reasons why the suggested program should have prompt and full study.

A Point Four Youth Corps would assure an adequate supply of young Americans to man public and private technical assistance missions in the years to come. But there are two even more important things to be said for it. Young Americans in their late teens and early twenties need a sense of purpose—the excitement and stimulus of taking part in great events. William James pointed this out a half century ago when he suggested in his essay "The Moral Equivalent of War" that a season on a fishing schooner or on a cattle ranch could well provide the sense of excitement and purpose which war—at least old-fashioned war— was supposed to provide. If the evolution of the have-not nations of Asia and Africa is at once the greatest challenge and adventure of the age, young Americans are going to want to become involved in it. Furthermore, from the standpoint of a successful American foreign policy, a Point Four Youth Corps could be equally beneficial.

Too often we seem to emphasize military alliances with corrupt or reactionary leaders; furnishing military hardware which all too frequently is turned on the people of the country we are presumably helping; grandiose and massive projects; hordes of American officials living aloof in enclaves in the country's capital. Would we not be farther along if we relied more heavily on a group of some thousands of young Americans willing to help with an irrigation project, digging a village well, or setting up a rural school?

The bills now before Congress (H.R. 9638 and S. 2908) sum up the objectives of the Point Four Youth Corps: first, to make additional technical manpower available to United States agencies and to private agencies carrying out economic, medical, educational, and community development programs in underdeveloped friendly countries; second, to assist in broadening the understanding by the peoples of other nations of the ideals and aspirations of Americans, through close contact with young Americans participating in the Point Four Youth Corps; third, to offer our young people an opportunity to serve their country in a stimulating way, while broadening their understanding of the problems facing other peoples and nations, and thereby helping them better to understand American policies and purposes abroad.

The bills would authorize a nongovernmental research group to conduct a study within one year of how best to organize the Point Four Youth Corps. The report would consider, first of all, the types of projects in which members of the Point Four Youth Corps might be used, based upon investigation of existing and proposed private and governmentally sponsored projects and their various goals. The study would also investigate the manner in which interested private American foundations, and groups, such as service clubs, religious groups, farm organizations, labor unions, business groups and similar organizations, might cooperate in the operation of Point Four Youth Corps projects and whether or not it would be desirable to provide that service in the Point Four Youth Corps be considered as satisfying the obligation of individuals to perform training and service in the Armed Forces. Also to be decided are questions on the optimum size of the Point Four Youth Corps, the period of service which might be required and the pay scales and conditions of employment which would be most desirable in the public interest and the pattern and manner of orientation and training in the United States and abroad that would be required to make young American adults effective workers in programs of technical cooperation. The study would also have to determine such questions as whether it would be practicable and advisable to recruit young American adults who have completed less than four years of college, whether the Point Four Youth Corps should be placed under the administration of a Federal agency or a private group on a contract basis, or both, and the manner in which the Point Four Youth Corps could most usefully supplement existing governmental and private programs of technical cooperation.

Although the program cannot be fully spelled out until all possibilities and pitfalls are studied, it might work in roughly this manner: John Farmer is draft-exempt while completing his agricultural course at the University of Wisconsin. After graduation he applies for a village-level job teaching modern farming methods as a member of the Point Four Youth Corps. If he is accepted, John gets perhaps a three-month stateside training period for his job and then is sent to a village project in India. He will be paid the wages and allowances he might have gotten in the Army. His hitch, like that of his rifle-toting counterpart, is for two years. Multiply his contribution by perhaps ten thousand, one number frequently mentioned for the Point Four Youth Corps, and you have an idea of its constructive possibilities. Such a massive injection of young blood would give a revolutionary boost to our Point Four programs in the under-developed nations in Latin America, Africa, the Middle East and South and Southeast Asia.

United States technical assistance already has proved its value in aiding the newly independent and desperately poor people of the world to help themselves. But, our Point Four program, after ten years, has displayed some critical weaknesses. The most obvious is that the United States program is but a drop in the bucket. There are now about six thousand Americans overseas on ICA [International Cooperation Administration, liquidated in 1961] projects. Ten times that number could be used in demonstrating better farming methods alone.

A second defect, which unfortunately seems inevitable in any government operation, is that our technical assistance programs are suffering from bureaucratic hardening of the arteries. Red tape and administrative paper work are keeping too many men and women tied to desks, leaving too few to get out in the field where they are most effective. Enlisting the cream of America's youth to work and teach in public and private technical assistance projects would go a long way to remedy these weaknesses.

Would such a program of sending qualified young American men and women abroad be too expensive? I don't think so. To be sure, it would cost money—perhaps $5,000 for each member of the Youth Corps including transportation and plain but adequate living facilities. On that basis, it would cost $50 million annually to send ten thousand young Americans abroad—only one thirtieth of the amount we are now spending on foreign economic aid. But if we can afford to send fifteen thousand United States Army officers and technicians to Turkey, one thousand to Iran and comparable numbers to such places as Pakistan, Laos and Vietnam to train soldiers, surely we can afford to send a much smaller number of young Americans to train farmers and teachers.

Fitting ten thousand serious-minded young men and women into present public and private technical assistance programs under the auspices of the Point Four Youth Corps is perfectly feasible. And the American slogan of "mutual aid" would be given real meaning if the young countries receiving the Point Four Youth Corps took pride in the fact that they were playing an important role in the training and education of young Americans. For their youth is the outstanding hope of many of these developing countries. Young men—and women—in their twenties and thirties are running everything from cabinet ministries to post offices, from schoolrooms to police forces.

This natural and unavoidable reliance on youth in countries from Guinea to Indonesia creates a sympathetic tie with young foreign visitors, American or otherwise. Almost invariably, it is the younger Americans in these countries who have made more friends and have had more influence among the people with whom they lived and worked. And yet most of our present Point Four technicians are in their forties, fifties and many in their sixties. The elders are frequently retired college professors, and the middle-aged are often Government agronomists or engineers on loan from the Department of Agriculture or Bureau of Roads.

These people are mature, experienced men and women. Their maturity and experience are needed to direct ICA programs in various countries, and most of them are doing a splendid job. But after forty-five it often gets harder to work up enthusiasm about living in an Arab mud house, sipping tea in an African grass hut or playing volleyball with Indian students. And just this sort of neighborly living abroad is necessary if we want to get our ideas across to farmers and peasants. The natives in Burma or Morocco are just as suspicious of "foreign ways" as are the natives in Wisconsin or Maine. . . .

One of the principal values of the bill to date has been to crystallize and channel support for such a program. My mail indicates tremendous eagerness on the part of our youth to enroll in the Point Four Youth Corps. The United States National Student Association, which represents some 1.3 million students in 375 colleges and universities, is busy mobilizing support for the Youth Corps program. The Harvard *Crimson* calls it "a very fine idea," and a group of Antioch College students have petitioned Senator J. William Fulbright [Democrat of Arkansas], chairman of the Senate Foreign Relations Committee, to act quickly and favorably on the proposal for the Youth Corps.

Furthermore, support has by no means been limited to students and student groups. An editorial in the *Christian Science Monitor* summed up its support this way:

> Mr. Reuss's plan would help show the emerging peoples in a personal way the American altruism that now is too often lost amidst dollar signs. It would strengthen language training, promote a more professional foreign service, and give enthusiastic young Americans a more mature understanding of the world they will have to face. In short, it merits bipartisan priority treatment.

Union leader Victor Reuther wrote that "your proposal can become a most important escape route from the rut in which American foreign policy and much of American domestic policy now jog along." And other individual endorsements have come from veterans who recall that their talents were either wasted or neglected in military service. All told, of the several hundred letters I have received from people in nearly every state and in several foreign countries, all but one favor the proposal. At least one leading university and a well-known foundation are considering undertaking the study of the Youth Corps. . . .

The sooner Congress acts, the better. It is among the have-not nations that the great game must be played in the coming generation, and money and military aid alone will not win. Moscow and Peking are carefully training cadres to go out into the villages. The authoritarian control they work under puts them at a disadvantage—but only if there are, on the scene, other workers who are both free and capable.

The Point Four Youth Corps offers us a means to put such workers on the spot, a means to demonstrate vividly the genuine and generous interest that Americans have in the well-being of developing nations and their people. [Congress passed the Reuss-Neuberger bill in June 1960, and under its provisions the Colorado State University Research Foundation investigated the feasibility of a Peace Corps—Ed.]

AN ALTERNATIVE TO MILITARY SERVICE [2]

Whoever our next President may be—whomever he selects as his Secretary of State—their efforts for a successful foreign policy, their efforts for peace, will depend in large measure on the men and women who must carry out that policy. A program for peace can be no better than those who implement it. Our stature abroad can be no more respected or influential than those who speak for us. The policies may be decided at the top—but they are planned and executed here, and accepted or rejected abroad, at a somewhat lower level. . . .

The hard, tough work of laying the groundwork for peace must be done by thousands of hands. It was Clemenceau who said: "War is much too serious a matter to be entrusted to the generals"—and surely, in this nuclear age, peace is much too serious a matter to be entrusted to either generals or summit conferences.

We can push a button to start the next war—but there is no push-button magic to bring a just and lasting peace. To be peace-loving is not enough—for the Sermon on the Mount saved its blessing for peacemakers. The generation for which I speak has seen enough of warmongers—let our great role in history be that of peacemakers.

But the harsh facts of the matter are that in three vital areas we have been ill-staffed and ill-represented in the struggle for peace—in our disarmament planning—in our diplomatic and foreign service—and in our technical assistance to underdeveloped nations.

In all three areas, we have failed to realize that times have changed since World War II. Weapons are more complex—and therefore so is their control. The enemy advances now by non-military methods—and military methods cannot prevent that advance. . . .

I want to turn now to the problems of our foreign policy staff overseas. Many Americans have marveled at the selfless example

[2] From presidential campaign speech delivered by the late President John F. Kennedy, then Senator from Massachusetts, November 2, 1960. Text from New York *Times*. p 32. N. 3, '60.

of Dr. Tom Dooley in Laos. Many have shuddered at the examples in *The Ugly American*. Both examples may be found in great numbers in our overseas missions. But most of our personnel are somewhere in between. Most could be doing a better job—and most must do a better job if we are to survive the modern techniques of conquest.

For on the other side of the globe, diplomats skilled in the languages and customs of the nation to whom they are accredited—teachers, doctors, technicians and experts desperately needed in a dozen fields by underdeveloped nations—are pouring forth from Moscow to advance the cause of world communism. The Lenin Institute for Political Warfare exports each year hundreds of agents to disrupt free institutions in the uncommitted world. A friend of mine visiting the Soviet Union last year met a young Russian couple studying Swahili and African customs at the Moscow Institute of Languages. They were not language teachers—he was a sanitation engineer and she was a nurse. And they were being prepared to live among African nations as missionaries for communism.

Already Asia has more of the Soviet than American technicians—and Africa may by this time. Russian diplomats are the first to arrive, the first to offer aid, the only ones represented by key officials at diplomatic receptions. They know the country, they speak the language—and in Guinea, Ghana, Laos and all over the globe, they are working fast and effectively. Missiles and arms cannot stop them—neither can American dollars. They can only be countered by Americans equally skilled and equally dedicated—and if I am elected, I ask you to help me find those Americans. . . .

Where are we going to obtain the technicians needed to work with the peoples of underdeveloped lands outside the normal diplomatic channels—and by technicians I include engineers, doctors, teachers, agricultural experts, specialists in public law, labor, taxation, civil service—all the skills necessary to establish a viable economy, a stable government and a decent standard of living.

A news item in this week's paper reported that "a group of Russian geologists, electrical engineers, architects and farming and fishing experts arrived in Ghana today to give technical advice." Another item described the potentiality for Castro-type or Communist exploitation in northeast Brazil, where intolerable living standards have reduced thousands to a starvation diet, and in two villages prevented a single baby from living beyond the age of twelve months. And still another item described unrest in the Caribbean island of Haiti, where (in 1950) 90 per cent of the population has never been taught how to read or write, and there is one doctor for every ten thousand people.

Think of the wonders skilled American personnel could work, building good will, building the peace. There is not enough money in all America to relieve the misery of the underdeveloped world in a giant and endless soup kitchen. But there is enough know-how and enough knowledgeable people to help those nations help themselves.

I therefore propose that our inadequate efforts in this area be supplemented by a "peace corps" of talented young men willing and able to service their country in this fashion for three years as an alternative to peace-time Selective Service—well qualified through rigorous standards—well trained in the language, skills and customs they will need to know—and directed and paid by the ICA Point Four agencies. We cannot discontinue training our young men as soldiers of war—but we also need them as ambassadors of peace.

This would be a volunteer corps—and volunteers would be sought among talented young women as well—and from every race and walk of life. For this nation is full of young people eager to serve the cause of peace in the most useful way.

I have met them on campaigns across the country. When I suggested at the University of Michigan lately that we needed young men and women willing to give up a few years to serve their country in this fashion, the students proposed a new organization to promote such an effort. Others have indicated a similar response—offering a tremendous pool of talent that could work modern miracles for peace in dozens of underdeveloped nations.

I am convinced that our young men and women, dedicated to freedom, are fully capable of overcoming the efforts of Mr. Khrushchev's missionaries who are dedicated to undermining that freedom.

These proposals offer no quick and easy solution to the problems of peace. But they are essential tools. "Give me a fulcrum," Archimedes is reported to have said, "and I will move the world." The tools I have suggested can be our fulcrum—it is here we take our stand—let us move the world down the road to peace.

A PERMANENT PEACE CORPS [3]

I recommend to the Congress the establishment of a permanent Peace Corps—a pool of trained American men and women sent overseas by the United States Government or through private organizations and institutions to help foreign countries meet their urgent needs for skilled manpower. [A permanent Peace Corps was authorized by Congress in September 1961.—Ed.]

I have today signed an Executive Order establishing a Peace Corps on a temporary pilot basis.

The temporary Peace Corps will be a source of information and experience to aid us in formulating more effective plans for a permanent organization. . . . This temporary Peace Corps is being established under existing authority in the Mutual Security Act and will be located in the Department of State. Its initial expenses will be paid from appropriations currently available for our foreign aid program.

Throughout the world the people of the newly developing nations are struggling for economic and social progress which reflects their deepest desires. Our own freedom, and the future of freedom around the world, depend, in a very real sense, on their ability to build growing and independent nations where men

[3] From message delivered by the late President John F. Kennedy to the House of Representatives on March 1, 1961. (H. Doc. no 98) United States. Congress. House of Representatives. 87th Congress, 1st session. Supt. of Docs. Washington D.C. 20025. '61. p 2733-4.

can live in dignity, liberated from the bonds of hunger, ignorance, and poverty.

One of the greatest obstacles to the achievement of this goal is the lack of trained men and women with the skill to teach the young and assist in the operation of development projects—men and women with the capacity to cope with the demands of swiftly evolving economies, and with the dedication to put that capacity to work in the villages, the mountains, the towns and the factories of dozens of struggling nations.

The vast task of economic development urgently requires skilled people to do the work of the society—to help teach in the schools, construct development projects, demonstrate modern methods of sanitation in the villages, and perform a hundred other tasks calling for training and advanced knowledge.

To meet this urgent need for skilled manpower we are proposing the establishment of a Peace Corps—an organization which will recruit and train American volunteers, sending them abroad to work with the people of other nations.

This organization will differ from existing assistance programs in that its members will supplement technical advisers by offering the specific skills needed by developing nations if they are to put technical advice to work. They will help provide the skilled manpower necessary to carry out the development projects planned by the host governments, acting at a working level and serving at great personal sacrifice. There is little doubt that the number of those who wish to serve will be far greater than our capacity to absorb them.

The Peace Corps or some similar approach has been strongly advocated by Senator [Hubert H.] Humphrey [Democrat of Minnesota], Representative [Henry S.] Reuss [Democrat of Wisconsin] and others in Congress. It has received strong support from universities, voluntary agencies, student groups, labor unions, and business and professional organizations.

Last session the Congress authorized a study of these possibilities. Preliminary reports of this study show that the Peace Corps is feasible, needed and wanted by many foreign countries.

[The study, completed in May 1961, was made by the Colorado State University Research Foundation—Ed.]

Most heartening of all, the initial reaction to this proposal has been an enthusiastic response by student groups, professional organizations and private citizens everywhere—a convincing demonstration that we have in this country an immense reservoir of dedicated men and women willing to devote their energies and time and toil to the cause of world peace and human progress.

Among the specific programs to which Peace Corps members can contribute are: teaching in primary and secondary schools, especially as part of national English-language teaching programs; participation in the world-wide program of malaria eradication; instruction and operation of public health and sanitation projects; aiding in village development through school construction and other programs; increasing rural agricultural productivity by assisting local farmers to use modern implements and techniques. The initial emphasis of these programs will be on teaching. Thus the Peace Corps members will be an effective means of implementing the development programs of the host countries—programs which our technical assistance operations have helped to formulate.

The Peace Corps will not be limited to the young, or to college graduates. All Americans who are qualified will be welcome to join this effort. But undoubtedly the corps will be made up primarily of young people as they complete their formal education.

Because one of the greatest resources of a free society is the strength and diversity of its private organizations and institutions much of the Peace Corps program will be carried out by these groups, financially assisted by the Federal Government.

Sources of Supply

Peace Corps personnel will be made available to developing nations in the following ways:

1. Through private voluntary agencies carrying on international assistance programs.

2. Through overseas programs of colleges and universities.

3. Through assistance programs of international agencies.

4. Through assistance programs of the United States Government.

5. Through new programs which the Peace Corps itself directly administers.

In the majority of cases the Peace Corps will assume the entire responsibility for recruitment, training and the development of overseas projects. In other cases it will make available a pool of trained applicants to private groups who are carrying out the projects approved by the Peace Corps.

In the case of Peace Corps programs conducted through voluntary agencies and universities, these private institutions will have the option of using the national recruitment system—the central pool of trained manpower—or developing recruitment systems of their own.

In all cases men and women recruited as a result of Federal assistance will be members of the Peace Corps and enrolled in the central organization. All private recruitment and training programs will adhere to Peace Corps standards as a condition of Federal assistance.

In all instances the men and women of the Peace Corps will go only to those countries where their services and skills are genuinely needed and desired. United States operations missions, supplemented where necessary by special Peace Corps teams, will consult with leaders in foreign countries in order to determine where Peace Corpsmen are needed, the types of jobs they can best fill, and the number of people who can be usefully employed. The Peace Corps will not supply personnel for marginal undertakings without a sound economic or social justification. In furnishing assistance through the Peace Corps careful regard will be given to the particular country's developmental priorities.

Membership in the Peace Corps will be open to all Americans, and applications will be available shortly. Where application is made directly to the Peace Corps—the vast majority of cases—they will be carefully screened to make sure that those who are selected can contribute to Peace Corps programs, and have the personal qualities which will enable them to represent the United States abroad with honor and dignity. In those cases where application is made directly to a private group, the same basic standards will be maintained. Each new recruit will receive a training and orientation period varying from six weeks to six months. This training will include courses in the culture and language of the country to which they are being sent and specialized training designed to increase the work skills of recruits. In some cases training will be conducted by participant agencies and universities in approved training programs. Other training programs will be conducted by the Peace Corps staff.

Length of service in the corps will vary depending on the kind of project and the country, generally ranging from two to three years. Peace Corps members will often serve under conditions of physical hardship, living under primitive conditions among the people of developing nations. For every Peace Corps member service will mean a great financial sacrifice. They will receive no salary. Instead they will be given an allowance which will only be sufficient to meet their basic needs and maintain health. It is essential that Peace Corpsmen and women live simply and unostentatiously among the people they have come to assist. At the conclusion of their tours, members of the Peace Corps will receive a small sum in the form of severance pay based on length of service abroad, to assist them during their first weeks back in the United States. Service with the Peace Corps will not exempt volunteers from Selective Service.

The United States will assume responsibility for supplying medical services to Peace Corps members and ensuring supplies and drugs necessary to good health. . . .

The benefits of the Peace Corps will not be limited to the countries in which it serves. Our own young men and women will be enriched by the experience of living and working in foreign lands. They will have acquired new skills and experience which will aid them in their future careers and add to our own country's supply of trained personnel and teachers. They will return better able to assume the responsibilities of American citizenship and with greater understanding of our global responsibilities.

Although this is an American Peace Corps, the problem of world development is not just an American problem. Let us hope that other nations will mobilize the spirit and energies and skill of their people in some form of Peace Corps—making our own effort only one step in a major international effort to increase the welfare of all men and improve understanding among nations.

THE MORAL EQUIVALENT OF WAR [4]

The war against war is going to be no holiday excursion or camping party. The military feelings are too deeply grounded to abdicate their place among our ideals until better substitutes are offered than the glory and shame that come to nations as well as to individuals from the ups and downs of politics and the vicissitudes of trade. There is something highly paradoxical in the modern man's relation to war. Ask all our millions, north and south, whether they would vote now (were such a thing possible) to have our war for the Union expunged from history, and the record of a peaceful transition to the present time substituted for that of its marches and battles, and probably hardly a handful of eccentrics would say yes. Those ancestors, those efforts, those memories and legends, are the most ideal part of what we now own together, a sacred spiritual possession worth more than all the blood poured out. Yet ask those same people whether they would be willing in cold blood to start another civil war now to gain another similar possession, and not one man or woman would vote for the proposition. In modern eyes . . . [wars] . . . must not be waged solely for the sake of the ideal harvest. Only when forced upon one, only when

[4] From essay in *Memories and Studies*, by William James, American philosopher. Longmans, Green, and Co. New York. '11. p 267-96. Copyright 1911 by Henry James, Jr. Reprinted by permission of Paul R. Reynolds, Inc., 599 Fifth Avenue, New York, N.Y. 10017.

an enemy's injustice leaves us no alternative, is a war now thought permissible.

It was not thus in ancient times. The earlier men were hunting men, and to hunt a neighboring tribe . . . was the most profitable, as well as the most exciting, way of living. . . .

Modern man inherits all the innate pugnacity and all the love of glory of his ancestors. Showing war's irrationality and horror is of no effect upon him. The horrors make the fascination. War is the *strong* life; it is life *in extremis;* war-taxes are the only ones men never hesitate to pay, as the budgets of all nations show us.

History is a bath of blood. . . . Let public opinion once reach a certain fighting pitch, and no ruler can withstand it. . . . It all seems to lead back to two unwillingnesses of the imagination, one aesthetic, and the other moral; unwillingness, first to envisage a future in which army-life, with its many elements of charm, shall be forever impossible, and in which the destinies of peoples shall nevermore be decided quickly, thrillingly, and tragically, by force, but only gradually and insipidly by "evolution"; and, secondly, unwillingness to see the supreme theater of human strenuousness closed, and the splendid military aptitudes of men doomed to keep always in a state of latency and never show themselves in action. These insistent unwillingnesses, no less than other aesthetic and ethical insistencies, have, it seems to me, to be listened to and respected. One cannot meet them effectively by mere counterinsistency on war's expensiveness and horror. The horror makes the thrill. . . .

I will now confess my own utopia. I devoutly believe in the reign of peace and in the gradual advent of some sort of a socialistic equilibrium. The fatalistic view of the war-function is to me nonsense, for I know that war-making is due to definite motives and subject to prudential checks and reasonable criticisms, just like any other form of enterprise. And when whole nations are the armies, and the science of destruction vies in intellectual refinement with the sciences of production, I see that war becomes absurd and impossible from its own monstrosity. Extravagant ambitions will have to be replaced by reasonable claims, and nations must make common cause against them. . . . I look forward to a future when acts of war shall be formally outlawed as between civilized peoples.

All these beliefs of mine put me squarely into the anti-militarist party. But I do not believe that peace either ought to be or will be permanent on this globe, unless the states pacifically organized preserve some of the old elements of army-discipline. A permanently successful peace-economy cannot be a simple pleasure-economy. In the more or less socialistic future toward which mankind seems drifting we must still subject ourselves collectively to those severities which answer to our real position upon this only partly hospitable globe. We must make new energies and hardihoods continue the manliness to which the military mind so faithfully clings. Martial virtues must be the enduring cement; intrepidity, contempt of softness, surrender of private interest, obedience to command, must still remain the rock upon which states are built—unless, indeed, we wish for dangerous reactions against commonwealths fit only for contempt, and liable to invite attack whenever a center of crystallization for military-minded enterprise gets formed anywhere in their neighborhood.

The war-party is assuredly right in affirming and reaffirming that the martial virtues, although originally gained by the race through war, are absolute and permanent human goods. Patriotic pride and ambition in their military form are, after all, only specifications of a more general competitive passion. They are its first form, but that is no reason for supposing them to be its last form. Men now are proud of belonging to a conquering nation, and without a murmur they lay down their persons and their wealth, if by so doing they may fend off subjection. But who can be sure that *other aspects of one's country* may not, with time and education and suggestion enough, come to be regarded with similarly effective feelings of pride and shame? Why should men not some day feel that it is worth a blood-tax to belong to a collectively superior in *any* ideal respect? Why should they not blush with indignant shame if the community that owns them is vile in any way whatsoever? Individuals, daily more numerous, now feel this civic passion. It is only a question of blowing on the spark till the whole population gets incandescent, and on the ruins of the old morals of military honor, a stable system of morals of civic honor builds itself up. What the whole community comes to believe in grasps the individual as in a vise. The war-function has grasped us so far; but constructive interests may some day seem no less imperative, and impose on the individual a hardly lighter burden.

Let me illustrate my idea more concretely. There is nothing to make one indignant in the mere fact that life is hard; that men should toil and suffer pain. The planetary conditions once for all are such, and we can stand it. But that so many men, by mere accidents of birth and opportunity, should have a life of *nothing else* but toil and pain and hardness and inferiority imposed upon them, should have *no* vacation, while others natively no more deserving never get any taste of this campaigning life at all,—*this* is capable of arousing indignation in reflective minds. It may end by seeming shameful to all of us that some of us have nothing but campaigning, and others nothing but unmanly ease. If now—and this is my idea—there were, instead of military conscription a conscription of the whole youthful population to form for a certain number of years a part of the army enlisted against *Nature,* the injustice would tend to be evened out, and numerous other goods to the commonwealth would follow. The military ideals of hardihood and discipline would be wrought into the growing fibre of the people; no one would remain blind as the luxurious classes now are blind, to man's relations to the globe he lives on, and to the permanently sour and hard foundations of his higher life. To coal and iron mines, to freight trains, to fishing fleets in December, to dishwashing, clothes-washing, and window-washing, to road-building and tunnel-making, to foundries and stoke-holes, and to the frames of skyscrapers, would our gilded youths be drafted off, according to their choice, to get the childishness knocked out of them, and to come back into society with healthier sympathies and soberer ideas. They would have paid their blood-tax, done their own part in the immemorial human warfare against nature; they would tread the earth more proudly, the women would value them more highly, they would be better fathers and teachers of the following generation.

Such a conscription, with the state of public opinion that would have required it, and the many moral fruits it would bear, would preserve in the midst of a pacific civilization the manly virtues which the military party is so afraid of seeing disappear in peace. We should get toughness without callousness, authority with as little criminal cruelty as possible, and painful work done cheerily because the duty is temporary, and threatens not, as now, to degrade the whole remainder of one's life. I spoke of the "moral equivalent" of war. So far, war has been the only force that can discipline a whole community, and until an equivalent discipline is organized, I believe that war must have its way. But I have no serious doubt that the ordinary prides and shames of social man, once developed to a certain intensity, are capable of organizing such a moral equivalent as I have sketched, or some other just as effective for preserving manliness of type. It is but a question of time, of skillful propagandism, and of opinion-making men seizing historic opportunities.

The martial type of character can be bred without war. Strenuous honor and disinterestedness abound elsewhere. Priests and medical men are in a fashion educated to it, and we should all feel some degree of it imperative if we were conscious of our work as an obligatory service to the state. We should be *owned,* as soldiers are by the army, and our pride would rise accordingly. We could be poor, then, without humiliation, as army officers now are. The only thing needed henceforward is to inflame the civic temper as past history has inflamed the military temper.

WORLD ORDER IN BEING [5]

World order will be, like science, like most inventions, a social product, an innumerable number of personalities will have

[5] From *The New World Order*, by H. G. Wells, the English author. Secker and Warburg. London. '40. p 161-91. Copyright 1940 by H. G. Wells. Reprinted by permission of the Executors of H. G. Wells and Messrs. Secker and Warburg.

lived fine lives, pouring their best into the collective achievement.
. . . There must be a multitude of young and youngish people
quite ripe for infection by this idea of cleaning up and resettling
the world. Young men who are now poring over war maps and
planning annexations and strategic boundaries, fresh Maginot
lines, new Gibraltars and Dardanelles, may presently be schem-
ing the happy and healthy distribution of routes and residential
districts in relation to this or that important region of world
supply for oil or wheat or water-power. It is essentially the same
type of cerebration, better employed.

Considerations of this sort are sufficient to supply a background of hopeful activities to our prospective world order. But
we are not all architects and gardeners; there are many types of
minds and many of those who are training or being trained for
the skilled cooperations of warfare and the development of a
combatant morale may be more disposed to go on with definitely
educational work. In that way they can most easily gratify the
craving for power and honorable service. They will face a world
in extreme need of more teachers and fresh-minded and inspiring
teachers at that. At every level of educational work from the
kindergarten to the research laboratory, and in every part of the
world from Capricornia to Alaska and from the Gold Coast to
Japan, there will be need of active workers to bring minds into
harmony with the new order and to work out, with all the labor-
saving and multiplying apparatus available, cinema, radio, cheap
books and pictures and all the rest of it, the endless new problems
of human liaison that will arise. There we have a second line of
work along which millions of young people may escape the
stagnation and frustration which closed in upon their pred-
ecessors as the old order drew to its end.

A sturdy and assertive variety of the new young will be
needed for the police work of the world. They will be more
disposed for authority and less for teaching or creative activities
than their fellows. The old proverb will still hold for the new
order that it takes all sorts to make a world, and the alternative
to driving this type of temperament into conspiracy and fighting
it and, if you can, suppressing it, is to employ it, win it over,

trust it, and give it law behind it to respect and enforce. They want a loyalty and this loyalty will find its best use and satisfaction in the service of world order. . . . Professor William James, in a small book entitled *The Moral Equivalent of War* . . . [see "The Moral Equivalent of War," above] pointed out the need there might be for a conception of duty, side by side with the idea of rights, that there should be something in the life of every citizen, man or woman alike, that should give him at once a sense of personal obligation to the World State and personal ownership in the World State. He brought that into relation with the fact that there will remain in any social order we can conceive, a multitude of necessary services which by no sort of device can be made attractive as normal lifelong occupations. He was not thinking so much of the fast-vanishing problem of mechanical toil as of such irksome tasks as the prison warder's, the asylum attendant's; the care of the aged and infirm, nursing generally, health and sanitary services, a certain residuum of clerical routine, dangerous exploration and experiment. No doubt human goodness is sufficient to supply volunteers for many of these things, but are the rest of us entitled to profit by their devotion? His solution is universal conscription for a certain period of the adult life. The young will have to do so much service and take so much risk for the general welfare as the world commonweal requires. They will be able to do these jobs with the freshness and vigor of those who know they will presently be released, and who find their honor in a thorough performance; they will not be subjected to that deadening temptation to self-protective slacking and mechanical insensitiveness, which assails all who are thrust by economic necessity into these callings for good and all.

It is quite possible that a certain percentage of these conscripts may be caught by the interest of what they are doing; the asylum attendant may decide to specialize in psychotherapeutic work; the hospital nurse succumb to that curiosity which underlies the great physiologist; the Arctic worker may fall in love with his snowy wilderness. . . .

PROMISE AND PROBLEMS OF A PEACE CORPS [6]

During the last presidential campaign, President John F. Kennedy proposed that the United States Government recruit a "peace corps" of talented young men and women, on a volunteer basis, to serve the cause of peace by working with the peoples of the underdeveloped world to help wipe out sickness, illiteracy, and hunger [See "An Alternative to Military Service," in this section, above.]

In his State of the Union message to Congress, of January 30, 1961, the President extended the concept:

> An even more valuable national asset (more valuable than surplus food) is our reservoir of dedicated men and women—not only on our college campuses but in every age group—who have indicated their desire to contribute their skills, their efforts, and a part of their lives to the fight for world order. We can mobilize this talent through the formation of a National Peace Corps, enlisting the services of all those with the desire and capacity to help foreign lands meet their urgent needs for trained personnel.

The "peace corps" proposal is not new, by itself. Similar ideas for Government programs have been advanced for fifty years. Private agencies have a long and successful record of activities of this kind. A bill to establish a United States Peace Corps was submitted to the Congress in June, 1960. Although that bill was not enacted, the 86th Congress did pass legislation authorizing a study of the advisability and practicability of establishing a Point Four Youth Corps.

But never before had a President endorsed the idea and made it an important part of his program. And President Kennedy's endorsement touched off a great wave of interest and enthusiasm on the part of young and older people alike. Young people saw here an opportunity to put their idealism into practice through direct service to the cause of peace. Older people saw this as an opportunity for expanded international action to build world peace and progress.

[6] From *An International Peace Corps. . .The Promise and Problems*, pamphlet by Samuel P. Hayes professor of economics, University of Michigan (1959-62), president, Foreign Policy Association (since 1962). Public Affairs Institute, 201 Massachusetts Ave., S.E. Washington, D.C. 20002. '61. p 8-10, 14-19. Reprinted by permission.

Some saw the Peace Corps as mainly an agency to help the nations of Africa, Asia and Latin America step up the pace of their economic and social development. Others saw in it a means of helping to train the youth of the United States and of other countries for responsible citizenship; or of building increased mutual understanding among peoples of different nations; or of helping the United States with some of its own problems of education and social welfare; or of training a pool of young people for later international careers.

But why should the *United States Government* establish and finance a program of volunteer service abroad? The reasons go to the very core of American national policy.

The ultimate objectives of American foreign policy, which is simply an extension of American national policy, are well known and thoroughly grounded in bipartisan agreement. We want a better life for our people. We want world conditions which will permit and will lead to such a better life. And for many of us, our own "better life" implies assurance that the other peoples of the world are coming to have a better life, too. For humanitarianism is a strong thread running through much that we do, both at home and abroad.

As we see it, achieving a "better life" for ourselves demands a world at peace, a world of increasing personal freedom and dignity for the individual, a world where the relations among men are governed by principles of justice (on which there is coming to be more and more international agreement), a world where material and cultural progress make increasingly possible the full development of personality and the achievement of individual aspirations. "Personal freedom" is, of course, a *necessary* but by no means *sufficient* condition for achieving individual aspirations.

These statements attempt to define the national objectives of the United States. It is tempting to assume that other nations place the same value on these objectives that the United States does. The assumption that peoples everywhere have the same goals is, however, erroneous. Other peoples may place a higher value on spiritual and intellectual experience, and less on political freedom and material prosperity than we do. They may feel that the needed pace of change justifies different attitudes toward civil rights and political processes. We should not seek to impose our values and goals on others, any more than we should accept their values and goals for ourselves. Where cooperative action can help both them and us to achieve *their and our goals*—and there are many areas of action that do in fact serve the goals of others as well as our own goals—there is opportunity for genuine international partnership.

Most nations of the world want economic and social development as a prerequisite to the attainment of their other goals. The United States, too, wants to see the rate of economic and social development stepped up, especially in the low income countries of Africa, Asia and Latin America. It is devoting large resources to helping such development, both directly and through international organizations. But more needs to be done.

There are many situations in the world where local and foreign resources of capital, of technology and of leadership could be far more productive than they are today, and make a far greater contribution to growth and development, if a missing element could be provided. That missing element is middle manpower. Unskilled manpower is usually plentiful. Top leadership can often be found. Equipment and expert advisers, if not locally available, can be brought in from abroad under existing aid programs. But a gap exists in the middle levels. For a generation, in many of the low income countries, there will be critical shortages of personnel with college, university and professional training, with teaching, craft, art, farming, organizing and leadership skills.

Our society has made a major investment in its people, and now has scores of millions of people with such training and skills. They help account for our own high productivity and level of living. They are critically needed in the low-income countries.

The central purpose of an International Peace Corps, and the reason why the United States Government should establish and finance it, is to help provide this missing element in the socio-economic structure of those nations that need it and want it to speed up their own development. This added element would supplement and make more fruitful the technical assistance, the educational opportunities, the economic aid, the private investment, which the higher-income countries are already providing. And, beyond its contribution to productivity alone, this added element would have great impact on the psychological and social changes that these low-income countries are seeking to bring about as their modernization advances.

Earlier Proposals and Other Programs

The idea that peaceful, constructive work might be organized for young men as an alternative to compulsory military service apparently goes back to the speech William James made before the Universal Peace Congress at Boston, in 1904. Later, he developed the idea further in an essay entitled *The Moral Equivalent of War* [see "The Moral Equivalent of War," in this section, above], where he discussed the need for an outlet for the aggressive impulses that he considered characterize our society. He proposed, as a way of rechanneling this aggression in a constructive direction, a youth peace army which would undertake adventuresome, dangerous projects, working under military-type discipline, but doing constructive work instead of military drills. . . .

Something of this kind took place in the Philippines in 1901, at the end of the Spanish-American War. American soldiers were given the option of being demobilized back to the United States or staying in the Philippines to become teachers in the educational system then being set up. Many of them stayed, going to the barrios [city and village districts] and living in the small one-room schoolhouses where they did their teaching. Thousands of Filipinos, including Ambassador [Carlos P.] Romulo, had their first teaching from a soldier-teacher.

The Civilian Conservation Corps was set up in 1933 under President Franklin D. Roosevelt. Under this program, young men worked on constructive social projects, living under a kind of military discipline. One of the motivations here, of course, was to find useful jobs for unemployed youth. The CCC made important contributions, both to the nation's social capital and to the forming of character among our young people.

There has been extensive experience in using youthful volunteers on international work camp projects. According to UNESCO, over 300,000 young volunteers from 41 countries are now participating each year in some kind of work camp activity. More than 125 agencies are in communication with UNESCO's "Coordination Committee for International Voluntary Work Camps."

Voluntary service programs, bringing young people of different nationalities together to work in action programs in this country and abroad, have been carried on by American private agencies for many years. For example, since 1917, the American Friends Service Committee has been engaged in the development and implementation of action programs of this sort. These programs have involved voluntary service on projects having the official and contractual cooperation of national governments at home and abroad. The programs have ranged from war relief and refugee resettlement, through general community development and mental health programs, to a particularized youth service program which was first initiated in 1934, and which has expanded rapidly since World War II. These youth programs now include community service and work camp programs in Europe, India, Africa, Japan and Mexico; seminars in Europe, Southeast Asia and the Far East; as well as domestic counterparts of all these programs.

A more recently established program is that of International Voluntary Services, Inc., a nonprofit corporation organized in 1953. It is nonsectarian, and is governed by members drawn from the top echelon of each of fifteen leading church denominations—one Catholic and fourteen Protestant. It was organized by people committed to the idea that American youth could make an important contribution to United States foreign policy by establishing person-to-person contacts with people of other countries, through a service program which the people of the host countries would want and in which they would participate.

During the past seven and a half years, IVS has conducted eleven projects in nine different countries (Egypt, Jordan, Iraq, Nepal, Laos, Vietnam, Cambodia, Ghana and Liberia). Eight of these projects have been operated under contract with ICA and three others under contracts and/or grants from various foundations. Under these contracts, personnel to the extent of approximately two hundred have been or are now associated with IVS. IVS volunteers have been mainly concerned with agricultural and village development, including teaching, health projects, road building and so forth.

A somewhat similar British group, Voluntary Service Overseas, began operations in 1958, when they sent fifteen volunteers abroad. In 1959 they sent sixty volunteers, and in 1960 they sent eighty-five volunteers overseas.

The National 4-H Club Foundation of America, Inc., has for a number of years carried on a program of International Farm Youth Exchange, with backing from the Cooperative Extension Service of the United States Department of Agriculture. Under this program, farm youths from America live with farm families and work in other countries for a period of time, and those from other countries live with farm families and work here.

AIESEC-US, which is the affiliate in the United States of The International Association of Students in Economics and Commerce, is a student-run organization which arranges opportunities for foreign students to get business training in companies in the United States, and for American students to get business training in companies in Europe, mostly during the summer holidays. Some 2,700 business training opportunities were arranged through this organization in 1960, of which 360 were arranged for Americans.

The University of California (Los Angeles) has for a number of years sent a dozen or so students on "Project India," during the summer vacation. They carry out a different work project in India each summer.

Operation Crossroads Africa, Inc., has for two summers sent fairly large groups of college students (180 in the summer of 1960) to Africa for joint work projects during the summer months.

There, American college students work side by side with African youths of similar age, on projects which require primarily manual labor. This program is well described by Gertrude Samuels in the New York *Times Magazine* of February 5, 1961. . . .

An imaginative proposal for using people with modest technical skills as teachers and operators—in addition to the high-level expert advisers—in the Point Four Program was made by Dewey Anderson and Stephen Raushenbush, in the *Bold New Program Series, No. 1, A Policy and Program for Success* (Washington: The Public Affairs Institute, 1950). Under this plan, 250 "Work Centers" would be established in underdeveloped countries over a six-year period, each staffed by:

. . . some ten people from the industrialized world with a variety of skills and some twenty local assistants who would, in time, take over. . . . Each of these centers would have enough equipment to teach people all that they could take and use about simple machines, agricultural and health practices. Each would have some scholarship funds to allow promising young people to stay there awhile as students.

The idea that the Government should put its resources behind a major program of youth service . . . has been revived and stated by a number of people in recent years. In a report made to the United States Department of State in October 1953, President A. Ray Olpin, of the University of Utah, just returned from a trip to Japan and around the world, proposed that the United States Government should:

. . . call a sizable number of young men on missions to Japan or other foreign countries for a two- or three-year period with no remuneration other than living expenses. It would be understood that these men were not career people and that after these few years of service the individuals would be expected to return to their homes. . . . In order to make certain that a quota of representatives of Americans of this kind could be available, it might be well to have the program coordinated with the Selective Service or Reserve Training programs. In lieu of military service for two or three years it might be advantageous to send selected individuals on civilian missions abroad, with the understanding that when they returned they would be assigned to the active reserve. . . . They could do very well what the people in the lower echelons of our State Department Foreign Service are now doing, for one thing. Better still, they could live with the people in foreign lands, study their language and traditions and customs, teach the people American customs and language, serve as teachers in the schools, could even work alongside foreign peoples in certain forms of employment.

. . . The columnist and lecturer, Max Lerner, has been advocating a kind of peace corps program for several years, as has Victor G. Reuther, of the UAW. General James M. Gavin . . . [former] ambassador to France, made a similar proposal in a speech at the Regional Advisory Council on Nuclear Energy on October 27, 1960, in Miami Beach. He then discussed the idea with President Kennedy, shortly before the "peace corps" proposal was made in San Francisco. During the presidential campaign, both President Kennedy and Under Secretary of State Chester Bowles made a number of speeches promoting this general concept.

Thus, the idea of an International Peace Corps, using volunteers for constructive service abroad, has a considerable history both of thought and experience. There is much on which to build a wise and effective program. While the idea and the activities proposed are not wholly new, there is novelty in lifting to a much higher level and to a much broader scope a type of activity which has so far been carried on mainly by a few voluntary agencies, with relatively modest financing. The prospect of a major new governmental program, undertaken as a matter of national policy, is different enough from what has gone on in the past to account for the wide enthusiasm that it has engendered.

II. RECRUITING, TRAINING, AND ORGANIZATION

EDITOR'S INTRODUCTION

Only a small fraction of our national budget is devoted to the Peace Corps. Compared with the huge sums of money and amounts of energy involved in the foreign economic and military aid programs, the funds and efforts expended on this agency seem insignificant. Yet, as noted in the excerpt below from Charles E. Wingenbach's book on the Peace Corps, a few qualified volunteers can have such an important impact upon a small country as to be considered a serious part of that nation's development program by its government. Obviously recruitment, training, and organization of volunteers must be carried out with maximum effectiveness if the corps is to live up to such expectations. Local conditions, climate, language, and social and cultural factors, on the one hand, and the educational, physical, and emotional qualifications of the candidates, on the other hand, must be carefully evaluated and then a rapid, concentrated program undertaken to train and equip the volunteers.

The second selection in this section is an official Peace Corps statement on recruiting, selection, training, and other operations. An actual example of a volunteer's training can be found in the account by a librarian of her preparation in the United States and overseas for an assignment in Pakistan. The section concludes with an examination by R. Sargent Shriver, Jr., director of the Peace Corps, of the role of American colleges and universities in training volunteers for duty abroad.

TRAINING IN ACTION—PROJECT TANGANYIKA [1]

The average American knows of Tanganyika only as the site of Henry Stanley's Lake Victoria and the fabled Mount Kiliman-

[1] From *The Peace Corps—Who, How and Where* by Charles E. Wingenbach, staff member, New York *Herald Tribune's* Washington Bureau. John Day. New York. '61. p 78-85. © 1961 by Charles E. Wingenbach. Reprinted from *The Peace Corps—Who, How and Where* by Charles E. Wingenbach by permission of The John Day Company, Inc., publisher.

jaro. This December [1961], however, the country becomes the twenty-second African nation to gain independence since World War II, and will assume a pivotal role in emerging Africa's political life.

Both the Peace Corps and Tanganyika's Prime Minister Julius Nyerere regard the project as a serious part of the country's development; the current three-year plan was specially redrafted to include Peace Corps assistance.

The economy of Tanganyika is primarily agricultural, yet only 9 per cent of her land is under cultivation. The job of the Peace Corps volunteers will be twofold. The four civil engineers and twenty surveyors will build small "feeder" roads to connect outlying farms with the marketplace, and they will participate in such major projects as the Mwanza/Musoma road, now being constructed through [United States] Development Loan Fund [abolished in 1961] assistance. Six geologists are to study the land and rock formations to provide detailed maps for future exploitation of the as yet untapped mineral resources. When field work is not feasible, the road builders will teach. Tanganykian apprentices, and the geologists will work in regional offices of the geological survey division of the Tanganyika government.

To prepare the volunteers for their two years in Tanganyika, the Peace Corps has set up a rigid 4½-month training program involving three separate phases.

TEXAS WESTERN COLLEGE, EL PASO, TEXAS
(Eight Weeks)

One of the primary reasons why Texas Western was chosen is that the terrain of southwest Texas is very much like Tanganyika. This is important because a full week has been given over to supervised field trips in which the prospective recruits put their skills to work.

The over-all director of the El Paso program is Dr. Clyde Kelsey, a Texas Western psychology professor, and the Peace

Corps is represented by Robert W. Iversen of Pennsylvania State College, an instructor in American studies and international affairs.

The staff assembled is an impressive one. The Tanganyikan area specialists are Professor James B. Christensen of Michigan's Wayne State University and Dr. Margaret Bates of Goddard College in Vermont. Professor Christensen is an anthropologist with extensive experience in West Africa and speaks fluent Swahili, Tanganyika's principal language. When he joined the El Paso training team, he brought along as training aids over 2,000 slides and movies that he shot in northern Tanganyika in recent years. Dr. Bates, meanwhile, is an Oxford Ph.D. and an expert on Tanganyikan politics. . . .

The surveyors and civil engineers among the volunteers are under the supervision of Texas Western and University of Texas staff experts, while Scots-born Daniel Harkin, a geologist seasoned by many years' work in Tanganyika, is geological instructor.

The training is divided roughly into 40 per cent technical, 25 per cent area studies, 15 per cent medical training and physical conditioning, 10 per cent American institutions and international affairs, and 10 per cent language training. Technical training is further divided into classroom, laboratory work, and the work-practice field trips. Area orientation, or Tanganyikan studies, includes lectures and discussion periods, films and assigned readings on the history, culture, politics and economic development plans of Tanganyika. Medical training involves first-aid and disease instruction, while about seventy hours of calisthenics and other exercises compose the physical conditioning. The language program is intensive, but its main purpose is to make the volunteer familiar with, not fluent in, Swahili to prepare him for the main course to come in Tanganyika.

That the training is no Sunday pleasure outing is emphasized to the would-be corpsman at once. First, he is greeted with a stiff physical examination, psychological testing, and a long series of vaccinations against local diseases. Every morning thereafter he is awakened at 5:30 to start a day that may not end until he has finished cramming at midnight for the next day's session.

On Sunday—if he is sufficiently dedicated—he will spend his day off in further studying, reading another book or listening to tapes in Swahili. And much of his "spare" time is spent in discussing the program and the prospects ahead with his fellow recruits.

Field Training Center, Puerto Rico
(Twenty-six Days)

Those who survive the El Paso training will proceed, after a brief respite, to Puerto Rico. There the Peace Corps has set up a camp twelve miles inland from the port of Arecibo. The site is one thousand feet above sea level in a mountain range and a dense rain forest.

For Peace Corps officials, Arecibo has four basic advantages:

1. *Climate*—a taste of what to expect.

2. *Community development program*—Puerto Rico, under Commonwealth Governor Luis Muñoz Marín, has established rural improvement work in around 350 villages.

3. *"Spartan living"*—staff and volunteers sleep in tents, and only the minimum necessary equipment will be available.

4. *Foreign language and culture situation*—living and working among a people who speak a different language and have different customs and foods.

Like El Paso, round-the-clock will be the order of the day. Peace Corps officials emphasize, however, that theirs is not a military-type "boot camp" training. What they hope to develop in the volunteers is an "inner discipline" and sheer physical and mental endurance. "The job," one instructor said, "is how to make these fellows realize they've got more in them than they ever dreamt. Of course, we have to work on the assumption that these guys already have something to start off with."

And a tough program it is. Physical conditioning will play a major part in toughening the trainees, and this is the task of Forrest Evashevsky, the athletic director for the University of Iowa who volunteered as a consultant with the Peace Corps. Under the general category of swimming come life-saving and survival techniques, as well as guiding a kayak through the swift-moving waters of local streams. Then there are the "rock-climbing" and aerial obstacle courses, which involve scaling nearby cliffs and climbing ropes across rivers and chasms. Soon after the volunteer arrives, he is treated to classroom studies of map and compass direction-finding, and that same evening he is taken into the jungle to make his own way back by a specified time the next morning.

Since the Tanganyika group will train in Puerto Rico during the hurricane season, their medical and survival training may come in handy. They will be given first-aid situations, during which they will discover simulated "wounded and dying" along jungle paths. Experts will judge their reaction and approach to the problem at hand. If the hurricane *does* hit the area, they will have to worry not only about their own survival, but also the rescue of the local villagers. Shelters will have to be constructed, food provided, and first aid and transport to nearby hospitals will have to be given those caught by the storm. Woven throughout the entire experience is the idea of service to others, rather than self-preservation.

In addition to a continuous, though less intensive, course in Swahili, the volunteer will have evening lectures, which will cover three areas:

1. *"Critical incident."*

2. *Current events*—includes discussion of the civil rights problem in the United States, the Cuban invasion, the U-2 incident and other U.S. policy questions, as well as the Hungarian Revolution, the Pasternak affair, etc. The object, Peace Corps officials say, is not to "brainwash" those we send to work overseas but to make them aware of the several sides to each question, in case they get involved in similar discussions.

3. *Human relations*—differences in individual and group relationships in a foreign country.

Of the three, the "critical incident" is perhaps the most important. How is the Peace Corpsman to react in a delicate situation? For example, the corpsman and his native work-associate, or counterpart, are sitting down and talking over a local brew. In comes an American contractor, frustrated by problems and tired by long days without sleep. He begins ranting and raving about everything in general and against Tanganyika in particular, and the corpsman tries without success to quiet him down or send him away. Instead, he only gets worse. Does the corpsman, as one consultant commented, crawl under the nearest table and try to pretend the embarrassing situation doesn't exist? Or does he grab the contractor by the collar and drag him away? These are the type of questions the corpsman will have to solve himself.

The training in Puerto Rico will not just involve theory or experiment, however. They will spend about $4\frac{1}{2}$ days participating in community development projects, not in large groups but in pairs. Each pair will be put aboard a *publico* (Puerto Rican bus) and go to an assigned village. There they will live with a Puerto Rican family and work in cooperation with and under the direction of the local community development chief. Whether they build pigsties or plan forest trails will be up to him.

Next in technical training is site improvement. Here experts take the trainees out into the forest, and they are graded on their choice of sites, culverts, assessing forest acreage, and other tests. This phase is a practical carry-over of the week-long El Paso field trip.

The final test of endurance consists of two hiking expeditions, the first for $1\frac{1}{2}$ days and the second for 3 days. The volunteers travel by foot for considerable distances along roads, trails and through forest maze. The reason for the Herculean nature of the effort is to force the volunteer to pit his wit and what he has learned so far against the unknown in order to survive.

The only casualties expected from such rigorous training are a case or two of dysentery, some sprains and bruises, perhaps a broken bone—and some of the trainees who will not be able to make the grade. Its object, however, is to assure that the Peace Corpsman will not only have been trained technically, but also that he will learn the real meaning and purpose of the Peace Corps.

NATURAL RESOURCES SCHOOL, TENGERU, TANGANYIKA
(Seven Weeks)

The government of Tanganyika has set up a training program of its own at this technical school located at the foot of Mount Kilimanjaro. Graduates of both El Paso and Arecibo will study Swahili four hours a day, listen to further orientation lectures on Tanganyika, and take part in supervised field work in their specialty. Most of the instructors will be Tanganyikan.

With that final phase of training behind them, Project Tanganyika will begin work on assignment.

OPERATIONS OF THE PEACE CORPS [2]

Recruitment

During its first two years, the Peace Corps has faced some recruitment problems. Early publicity seemed to cause some confusion: many liberal arts graduates assumed one needed a technical skill—like the surveyors shown in recruitment brochures—to become a volunteer. Conversely, some farmers and skilled workers thought a college degree was a prerequisite to joining the Peace Corps. . . .

The Peace Corps has no recruiting stations scattered across the country and no personnel assigned exclusively to speechmaking. Volunteer workers handle most of the job. Teams from Washington composed of Peace Corps staff members backstop the volunteer workers with visits to the nation's colleges and universities. Other teams recruit for specialized skills in the nation's technical schools and 4-H organizations, at Grange meetings, factories and union halls. . . .

During the past fiscal year, the Peace Corps received 32,805 questionnaires from individuals wanting to serve as volunteers—and as the Peace Corps story becomes even better known, the total is mounting.

[2] From *Peace Corps; 2nd Annual Report.* United States. Peace Corps. Office of Public Affairs. Washington, D.C. 20525. 1963. p 34-41.

Selection

In selecting the best possible candidates for overseas service, the Peace Corps faces sometimes conflicting pressures. There are the requests from abroad for thousands and thousands of volunteers—many more than can be furnished. On the other hand, there are the thousands of applications from Americans who are willing and anxious to serve. Against these considerations, the Peace Corps must place its own desire to improve and tighten selection standards and overseas performance.

In two years, more than 58,000 persons filed formal applications to become volunteers. Of those who make formal application, about 25 to 30 per cent—more than one in four—are invited for training. About half of those invited (56 per cent) accept the invitation and enter training. This ratio has been growing. Four out of five trainees are selected for duty overseas. Thus, only one out of eight or nine of the original applicants actually becomes a Peace Corps volunteer in an overseas post.

In the selection process, letters of reference and other required information, including results of Peace Corps placement tests, are gathered, and assessment specialists spend an average of two hours reviewing, evaluating and doing further research, when necessary, on each application. . . .

When the Program Office calls for volunteers for a specific program, the Selection Division's classification section matches job specifications with individual applicant qualifications. Invitations to training are sent out and, for those who accept, a formal background check is conducted.

Selection continues during training under the guidance of a Peace Corps field selection officer assigned to each project. Trainees undergo a battery of psychological tests. Each is interviewed by psychiatrists and other assessment specialists. Trainees are told frankly about the problems and hardships they will encounter in the field. Some come to the difficult but honest conclusion that they would not be able to serve effectively and resign.

Advisory Selection Boards composed of Peace Corps staff members concerned with selection, training, and program development and—where appropriate—representatives of the administering private agency or university meet once in the middle of the training program and again at the end to recommend which trainees will be sent overseas as Peace Corps volunteers.

Selection has made a number of improvements in these various operations as the result of research and field experience showing what kind of person makes a successful volunteer. For example, greater stress is being placed upon language aptitude tests. Assessment experts are more precise in their judgment of applicant skills and more stringent in matching these skills to overseas needs. The trend is toward tighter requirements for more highly qualified volunteers.

Training

Peace Corps training remains a continuing experience in pressure-cooked education. New approaches are constantly being tried to improve the preparation of volunteers for overseas service. . . .

Training programs generally run eight to twelve weeks. Volunteers go through a sixty-hour week, Mondays through Saturdays, with evenings and Sundays often devoted to study, extra classes or field trips. . . .

Knowledge of the language spoken in the host country was early recognized as essential. The Peace Corps has made some special pioneering efforts in this field. We now have taught some forty languages, including Pushtu, Farsi, Krio, Twi, Tagalog. On the basis of experience and recommendations from volunteers in the field, we have increased, sometimes even doubled, language training so that it now takes up to 50 per cent of our total training time.

The Peace Corps has also made increasing efforts to make its training as realistic as possible, to give volunteers a "feel" of the situation they will face. Trainees bound for social work in Colombian city slums were given on-the-job training in New York City's Spanish Harlem. A group for Nepal was trained outdoors in mountainous Colorado. New Mexican Indian reservations and Spanish-speaking villages make realistic workshops for community development trainees. Puerto Rico provides experience in living in a Latin American environment. The Island of Hawaii, with its multiracial population, remote valleys and varied rural economy, performs a similar function for volunteers headed for Southeast Asia.

Because they discovered on arrival in their host country that some anticipated jobs had changed or been abolished, volunteers have had to be prepared to face the unexpected, and to be trained for a general job situation of variable possibilities.

Peace Corps training is a mixture of academic, technical, and cross-cultural studies. It is, at once, less and more than the standard college course. The Peace Corps may teach trainees how to build a school, but they must also know French or a local African tongue to work with their coworkers. A school teacher trainee should know some linguistics in order to help in English instruction, but he also should know the games his students will play and perhaps how to organize young people to dig fish ponds or latrines after class hours. A volunteer who travels by canoe should know how to swim as well as how to organize 4-H clubs and teach community health. . . .

In its efforts to meet the variety of needs in volunteer training, the Peace Corps has set up some special programs, including the two camps in Puerto Rico designed to give the volunteer a realistic idea of his own capacity and endurance in the face of new and continued challenge.

Activities at these camps include out-of-doors training ranging from rock-climbing to drownproofing to survival techniques. Volunteers live four to six days with rural Puerto Rican families. The Commonwealth of Puerto Rico provides volunteers with field work experience in community education, health, welfare, agriculture and housing.

The Peace Corps has concentrated its 26-day Puerto Rico conditioning program on volunteers headed for Latin America. In 1963, a modified version of the Puerto Rico facilities was established on the Island of Hawaii in connection with the University of Hawaii's Hilo Peace Corps training operation.

The Peace Corps has contracted with the University of New Mexico for a year-round training program in community development, which began in February of 1963, and was the first year-long training cycle conducted at a single institution. The New Mexico operation can handle 850 trainees a year in 12-week community development programs. Incorporated in this training is much of the "Outward Bound" camp experience other volunteers receive in Puerto Rico.

Operations Overseas

While the heart of the Peace Corps is the individual volunteer working in a community overseas, the major element in placement, support and guidance is located in the Office of Program Development and Operations. This office includes divisions in Washington and the staff overseas, the Peace Corps representative and his assistants in host countries. . . .

In the past year, Peace Corps programing has explored some new types of projects, such as urban community development, which has volunteers working in the crowded slums of cities in Chile, Ecuador, Venezuela, Colombia and Peru. Challenging opportunities were opened in the field of higher education and the Peace Corps responded by sending 274 volunteers to teach in the universities of 13 countries.

There has also been a re-emphasis on the need to provide manpower at the middle level between basic manual labor and highly developed skills. Professionally trained volunteers—doctors, graduate engineers, geologists—will continue to be used in special situations, but the core of Peace Corps work is in the middle manpower range. . . .

"Generalists" with college training in liberal arts comprise the single largest group (somewhat less than half) of all Peace Corps applicants, and ways of better utilizing their talents are being explored. Generalists can be highly effective in community action programs where they must awaken people to the possibilities for progress. They also serve in many Peace Corps teaching programs.

Staffing

To find capable people for the demanding overseas service, the Peace Corps conducts a far-ranging "talent search." Through a series of nation-wide contacts and recommendations, it locates and seeks to interest persons highly desirable for staff service abroad, and brings them to Washington for an exhaustive series of interviews with senior staff members. Peace Corps Director Shriver conducts the final interview and makes the final decision in every case.

In the past two years, more than 1,200 persons were processed through the talent search for overseas jobs. Fewer than one in six was hired. Those approved for hiring went through a series of security clearances and medical examinations. Their average age was 37. . . .

The ratio of total Peace Corps American staff (overseas and at home) to the number of trainees and volunteers decreased from 1 to 3.8 in June of 1962 to about 1 to 7 a year later. This ratio is still dropping toward a projected figure of 1 to 10 set as a goal to be attained when the number of Peace Corps volunteers reaches 10,000.

Overseas staff in a country usually consists of a Peace Corps representative, a doctor, a secretary, and one or more associate representatives. Foreign nationals are employed to the extent necessary to assist the staff. The Peace Corps representative and associates spend about half their time visiting volunteers at their work sites. The overseas staff receives no post differentials, no PX privileges, and no diplomatic privileges or immunities, except from certain taxes and duties. The housing is modest. The staff associates as much as possible with citizens of the host country.

University, Private and International Cooperation

The Peace Corps continues to involve other organizations— national and international, public and private—in its work. Such organizations have contracted to assist projects involving almost 30 per cent of the volunteers now in service or training.

Traditional voluntary groups such as the Young Women's Christian Association, CARE and Heifer, Project, Inc.; professional and trade associations like the American Association for Health, Physical Education and Recreation, and the Cooperative League of the U.S.A.; the great national farm organizations such as the Grange, the National Farmers' Union and the National 4-H Club Foundation are among those assisting the Peace Corps in 22 countries.

In addition, the Peace Corps is receiving assistance in overseas administration from 13 colleges and universities in 16 programs in 13 countries. Hundreds of volunteers benefit from the leadership and guidance of a faculty member or some other representative appointed by a university for his particular technical qualifications. . . .

These partnerships have not only enhanced the Peace Corps operation, but have stimulated and inspired private organizations in their overseas work.

Other private organizations, such as the Catholic Relief Services, the National Council of Churches, and the National Education Association, have established special offices to provide information to their members about the Peace Corps. [The Peace Corps, however, does not enter into contracts with church boards and agencies.]

Congress authorized the assignment of 125 Peace Corps volunteers to temporary duty with international organizations. Volunteers are working under the supervision of the [United Nations] Food and Agriculture Organization in Pakistan and Tunisia. Other projects with FAO guidance are planned for Colombia and Brazil.

Most host country governments have offered some form of assistance to the Peace Corps programs. A few pay part or all of the volunteers' living allowances. Many provide in-country transportation and medical care; others have made office space and clerical help available.

Individuals, foundations, clubs, school groups, organizations and business firms have given material support—books, tools and other equipment. CARE, for example, has donated more than $200,000 worth of equipment to Peace Corps programs. Heifer has made available some $90,000 worth of livestock.

The Asia Foundation has donated schoolbooks, and medical and laboratory equipment. The American Society of Peru gave money for the construction of two public buildings in Lima and Arequipa. United Nations agencies such as UNICEF and the FAO have donated fishing gear, microscopes and jeeps. Similar help for the Peace Corps has come from countless other organizations.

LIBRARIAN IN THE PEACE CORPS [3]

The Peace Corps librarian at the East Pakistan Academy for Village Development has her office in with the Women's Program office. In this country of Islam and purdah and the barely emerging female, just being a woman takes as much time as being a librarian. There are twenty-nine in the Peace Corps contingent assigned to East Pakistan and of the eight of us in Comilla at the Academy, two are women. The other girl is initiating a program with village women and I am working on extending library facilities to the villages.

The East Pakistan Peace Corps group began training the last week in August 1961 in Putney, Vermont. Putney is the national headquarters of the Experiment in International Living, which ran our training program under contract with the Peace Corps and is helping administer us in the field. Our East Pakistan group was the first to be assigned in Asia, as well as the first multipurpose group. The groups trained before us at Putney had been all engineers, all teachers, etc. Our professions range from carpenters and bricklayers to college teachers, so that it was impossible to give us any specialized training in our fields as they would apply in the country to which we were going.

Our training day was from eight in the morning until nine in the evening, six days a week. We studied Bengali, the language spoken in East Pakistan, for between four and six hours a day. Bengali is a proud literary language, one of its most illustrious

[3] From article by Jean Ellickson, librarian formerly with University of Michigan's Dearborn Center. *Wilson Library Bulletin.* 36:833-4. Je. '62.

recent spokesmen being Rabindranath Tagore. Though most of the educated Pakistanis speak English, they consider it a compliment for foreigners to learn their language.

The remainder of the day during our training period consisted of lectures on various aspects of East Pakistan, the problems of adapting to a foreign culture and discussions of our own culture. It has been said that one must know one's own country well before attempting to know another. However, we found it hard to concentrate on a rehashing of our own history when what we wanted most was to learn all we could about this new and exciting place, East Pakistan. A small library was set up for our benefit, but we were given no time to read in this tight schedule. It was decided we would have to do the reading we had been stimulated to do when we arrived in East Pakistan.

We arrived in Dacca, East Pakistan on October 28. Because of our sponsorship by the Experiment in International Living, an agency which arranges foreign tours and visits with local families for young people, we spent our first month living with a Pakistani family in Dacca, the provincial capital. We ate the same food, did the same things and in some cases slept in the same room with the rest of the family. We all had our problems with the initial change of diet, but since then we have remained in surprising good health. I say surprising because of the dire predictions of ill health both before we left the United States and from the American community here in Pakistan.

After our home stay we spent three more weeks in training before we took over our job assignments. This training took place at the Academy for Village Development, where I am now assigned. The initial purpose of the Academy was to retrain civil servants to operate effectively under the new Basic Democracies system of local government. In conjunction with this it was decided to give the Academy an extension function. Farmers' cooperatives were set up and in time all facets of village life will be worked on at the Academy. Our Peace Corps group was taken into training as another group to be shown village life, to learn what some of the problems are and incidentally to see what cooperation can do for villagers.

Eight of us stayed at the Academy for our work assignments. In addition to the girl in the women's program and myself, there are a tractor mechanic, a mechanical engineer, an agricultural extension worker, an irrigation engineer, a youth worker and a photographer working in the audio-visual department. Some of the Peace Corps volunteers in other parts of East Pakistan are having difficulty settling into their positions. The problem seems to be that officials in various institutions have requested that volunteers be sent to them, but have failed to explain to their personnel, with whom the volunteers will work, just what the volunteer's position should be. Some of this stems from the fact that, though the United States in the past has sent many advisers in supervisory positions, rarely have we sent technicians to work directly with the people. The Peace Corps is a fairly new concept and must make its own way as it goes along. There has been little difficulty in definition of position at the Academy, however. Almost from the moment we began our assignment in the middle of December, we have felt ourselves to be a part of the institution.

There is a library at the Academy which contains primarily rural sociology and community development materials for the use of the faculty and trainees. The librarian here has had the advantages of previous experience with a local USIS [United States Information Service] library, and had an American library consultant at the Academy for six months, though he has had no formal library training. However, I will not be working in the academic library, except in setting up better communications with other community development agencies around the world and abstracting whatever material we receive from them.

My major task is trying to extend library services into the villages. All the traditional problems come into play here. Not only is there the problem of how best to disseminate books, but there is a lack of books in Bengali and an absence of the reading habit among the villagers. The problem of adult literacy is being attacked on a variety of levels. However, only now is an attempt being made to coordinate these efforts. On a recent trip to Dacca, I was surprised at the number of agencies, both private and governmental, which are working on the problems of literacy and literature for the newly literate. But few of these agencies knew what the others were doing. I feel that it will be useful if I do nothing more than get these people to communicate and cooperate.

The Academy feels, and perhaps rightly so, that one of a librarian's duties should be to see that there are books in existence. I have been put in charge of the production of one hundred booklets for the newly literate. My first month here was spent writing for information and samples to agencies in other countries, which produce this type of material. The booklets we produce will be written simply and in story form, telling the villager how to do things by improved methods. Since the educated Pakistani tends to write flowery prose, the publications will be first written by me in English and then translated into Bengali. . . .

An attempt has been made to set up libraries in the villages before. There was a bookrack placed in one of the village homes in each of eleven villages, and these were supplied with all the extension publications of the Academy, a weekly newspaper of agricultural news and some books from the Academy's small circulating library. This initial attempt failed for a number of reasons, including the fact that, since the books were in one man's house, others did not feel free to come. We are now going to concentrate our efforts on getting books into the schools: primary, secondary and adult education centers. One of the problems we face here is that, especially in the case of primary schools, the buildings are often not even enough to keep the weather out.

Right now the volunteer's main preoccupation is just going out into the villages. Whenever a female corps member goes out, female heads soon peek out, and the women motion for us to come into their compounds. There they swarm around us and want to know why we aren't married, why we have short hair and why we don't wear jewelry as they do. I recently bought myself a set of glass bangle bracelets, like the local women wear, to avoid this last question. . . . The women always offer us tea and sweets (which they can barely afford to do) and the children sometimes give us flower leis made of marigolds. We have grown very fond of the village people of Pakistan in a very short time and hope that we can do something in return for them.

THE FIRST YEAR WAS TOUGH [4]

A year ago tonight, the Peace Corps was just six days old. And just a year ago, at your 1961 meeting, this association had the courage, the faith and the foresight to pledge its support to our fledgling enterprise.

So, tonight I especially welcome the opportunity to participate in your Conference on Higher Education. It's a pleasure to report that you backed a winner.

Three months ago I might have hesitated to make that statement. But when [Senator] Barry Goldwater [Republican of Arizona] endorsed the Peace Corps, I knew we were home free. Do you remember his candid comment?

I think the Peace Corps is beginning to remove the doubts from the doubters' minds. I have been impressed with the quality of the young men and women that have been going into it. At first, I thought that it would be advance work for a group of beatniks, but this is not so. As a businessman, I know that the two years' overseas experience will be invaluable and rewarding. I'll back it all the way.

He has since been joined by the Republican keynoter, [Representative] Walter Judd [Republican of Minnesota]. Tomorrow I expect [Representative] Charlie Halleck [Republican of Indiana] to announce that he has joined the majority of the Republican Party which voted for the Peace Corps when it was first proposed in the Congress. Most people don't remember that fact —that the majority of the Republicans in the House of Representatives voted for the Peace Corps last fall. They did, and it's important. Their support made the Peace Corps a truly national enterprise—not a partisan political endeavor.

[4] From address, "The Job Was Tough," delivered by R. Sargent Shriver, Jr., director of the Peace Corps, before the 17th National Conference on Higher Education, Chicago, March 6, 1962. *Vital Speeches of the Day.* 28:407-11. Ap. 15, '62. Reprinted by permission.

The President's Message to Congress establishing the Peace Corps called for a pool of trained Americans—volunteers to go overseas for the United States Government, to help foreign countries meet their urgent needs for skilled manpower.

A particular kind of person was required. That person had to have the physical and intellectual capacity to cope with the demands of swiftly evolving economies, the dedication to put that capacity to work—and to keep it working—in remote villages, in mountain areas, in towns, in factories, and in the schools of dozens of struggling nations. For them, the "age of revolutions" would mean service abroad—the new frontier for international education.

The job of the Peace Corps was tough. Some said it was impossible. Yet in the past year, the Peace Corps has recruited, selected, and trained more than nine hundred volunteers. They are already at work in twelve countries. . . .

That record is ours. But it is also yours.

It could not have been written without the full cooperation of colleges and universities. . . .

But the skeptics are still with us. Even though their initial doubts have not been fulfilled, they still have their nagging questions:

"What difference," they say, "does all this success mean? What you are doing is just a drop in the bucket. In the long sweep of history no one will remember whether the Peace Corps existed or didn't exist. Its influence will be negligible. Time, energy, and money will have been expended, but the results will be unimportant.

"Go ahead with your idealistic ventures," they say. "Americans have always oversimplified foreign affairs. The Peace Corps is no exception. Waste your money and your energies, but don't expect us to attach much significance to your effort."

Fortunately, all the experts are not skeptics.

Last week Arnold Toynbee wrote these words about the Peace Corps:

Here is a movement . . . whose express purpose is to overcome the disastrous barriers that have hitherto segregated the affluent Western minority of the human race from the majority of their fellow men and women. And the initiative in this has come from the country that is now the recognized leader of the Western world. Service in the Peace Corps [he goes on] is not an easy option. It calls for adventurousness, adaptability, human feeling, and, above all, self-sacrifice. There is something in human nature that responds to a challenge like this. I believe that, in the Peace Corps, the non-Western majority of mankind is going to meet a sample of Western Man at his best.

It was encouraging for us at the Peace Corps to read what Arnold Toynbee wrote. We have pondered over his words. Why does Mr. Toynbee say that Peace Corps volunteers will give an example of Western Man at his best?

I have no private insight into the great historian's mind, but tonight I'd like to venture a couple of guesses about his thoughts.

First, I think that he, like Barry Goldwater, must have been impressed by the quality of the volunteers he has seen. Mr. Toynbee visited the Peace Corps overseas training center in Puerto Rico. He spent two or three days talking to the volunteers, living with them, eating with them. . . .

I think Mr. Toynbee has probably been impressed also by the highly concentrated, effective education which we, with your help, have given to the volunteers. . . .

This summer we will have some thirty Peace Corps training programs being conducted simultaneously on campuses throughout the United States. In every one of these training programs the universities of America have marshaled unrivaled resources for instructing young Americans, and older ones, too, in the languages of the foreign countries, in the history, customs, traditions of the foreign countries; in world affairs, in American studies, in physical education and health education, as well as in professional fields such as teaching, engineering, geology, agriculture extension and nursing. No other country in the world could have mounted such specialized courses on such short order. And we already have dramatic evidence of the effectiveness of this effort made by American higher education on behalf of the Peace Corps.

Yesterday in Washington, the visiting foreign minister of Thailand and his colleagues told us that the recent group of

Peace Corps volunteers who arrived in Thailand had stunned the people and the officials of that country by their facility in speaking the Thai language, and by their knowledge of Thai history and traditions. Never before, he said, had any group of Americans arrived in his country as well prepared for their work.

The USIA stated that the most effective, single piece of news favorable to America in the last months in Thailand had been the advent in that country of the Peace Corps contingent, speaking Thai, singing Thai songs, knowing Thai history.

The University of Michigan created this special course in Thai culture and customs and language. For three months our volunteers worked twelve hours a day, six days a week. That's the reason why they were enthusiastically welcomed in Thailand. That's the reason why their work in that country will be successful.

At Ohio State, the Peace Corps trained a group destined for agricultural work in the Punjab region of India. The Dean of the School of Agriculture at that great university told me personally that the fully packed training schedule—sixty-six hours a week long—gave to the Peace Corps volunteers at Ohio State almost the equivalent of a full year's graduate work.

The minister of economic planning for the Punjab region, a distinguished Indian civil servant, came to this country, spent two weeks at Ohio State, and on his return to India stopped by in Washington specifically to congratulate Ohio State and the Peace Corps on the thoroughness and skill which he had observed in the training program at that institution.

I could easily go on. Our first training program, for example, at Texas Western College where we trained volunteers for Tanganyika was the subject of much skepticism in this country, and overseas the Tanganyikan government had some doubts that we could actually train people effectively for service in that remote African nation; so they sent the minister of communications and public works to our country and he spent ten days at Texas Western College in El Paso observing the volunteers and their study program.

Tanganyika originally asked for twenty-five people, but after this British civil servant saw the quality of the people and the kind of program of training, he came to Washington and asked us to send every one of the thirty-five volunteers to his country. Today, in fact, all of those Texas Western volunteers are in Tanganyika. They have been there seven months, and not one complaint has been lodged against them by the government or by the people of that important African nation.

I think Arnold Toynbee was thinking of these kinds of training programs when he said that the Peace Corps would send to the non-Western world examples of Western Man at his best.

Toynbee may also have been thinking of certain other qualities of the Peace Corps volunteers and the program under which they're serving. I mean—some of the psychological factors involved.

A Peace Corps volunteer arrives in a foreign country not only speaking the language of that country and knowledgeable about its customs and traditions, but he comes ready, willing and able to live the way they live, under *their* laws.

He does *not* try to change their religion.

He does *not* seek to make a profit from conducting business in their country.

He does *not* interfere in their political or military affairs.

He works within *their* system for *them*.

He helps to fill *their* needs as *they* see them.

He arrives on schedule.

In Ghana three of the first fifty-one teachers sent to the high schools of that country by the Peace Corps were elected assistant principal, or principal, of the schools to which they were assigned within four months of their arrival on the scene.

How many times in recent months have you heard of black men in Africa electing white men to positions of authority?

I suggest the Ghanaians were happy to accord these positions of influence to Peace Corps volunteers because the volunteers came to Ghana asking nothing, demanding nothing, except an opportunity to serve. They were not hanging around the PX commissary. In fact, they are excluded from such American perquisites.

They were not concentrated in the capital of that country, Accra. They were 300 miles up country in Tamale—250 miles to the west in Half Assini—450 miles away in Navrongo flush against the border of Upper Volta.

In Sierra Leone, when the volunteers disembarked in Freetown, they were not surprised to see a small group of officials waiting for them. This has become rather customary. But they were surprised when, as they walked up the streets of Freetown, the local inhabitants came out and stared at them as they went by. Only later did they discover the real reason for the unusual turnout of local inhabitants:

The inhabitants of Sierra Leone had never seen a white man walking up the street carrying his own luggage.

Once more, I suggest that Arnold Toynbee may be thinking of small, but significant, psychological factors such as these.

These Peace Corps volunteers are clearly *different* Americans. These facts explain more eloquently than any words I can command why it is that every one of the twelve countries to which the Peace Corps has sent volunteers has requested more of the same.

Over and above these factors, let me speculate for just a few minutes on another aspect of Peace Corps service abroad which may have been in Mr. Toynbee's mind and which will, I hope, be of interest to you.

The Peace Corps is attempting to communicate, humbly and compassionately, in the many languages of man—not just the spoken languages like French, Spanish, Urdu, Hindi, Swahili, or Tagalog—but the languages of poetry, of music, of law, of science, of painting and of teaching—the myriad methods by which man has learned to communicate his inmost thoughts and sensitivies to his fellow creatures. Let me illustrate what I mean:

We have sent five hundred teachers overseas, most of them secondary school teachers. We brought one of them back because he refused to participate in the social and recreational life of

Nigeria. He wanted to be only a teacher. But we're not sending people overseas who want to be only teachers. Formal education is one method of communicating the culture of past centuries to upcoming generations. It is essential. But a teacher whose role is restricted to the classroom is like a fighter with one hand tied behind his back. Our Peace Corps teachers must be human beings who participate in the full life of a foreign country, who communicate the substance of our culture on the playing field, in a social gathering, yes, even at a dance.

When the English said that the battle of Waterloo was won on the playing fields of Eton, they meant it. The battle of Africa may be won on the athletic fields of Ibadan University, just as much as in the classroom.

We have sent doctors overseas, and nurses, and nurse's aides, and we want to send many more. But we haven't sent any doctor whose idea of medical practice is restricted to large fees and comfortable office hours. A Peace Corps doctor is a man or woman who has voluntarily surrendered the high income which every doctor in our country can now command and in its place has accepted a different sort of reward. One of them expressed it to me in these words:

The future of my children may be determined more by what happens in Africa, South of the Sahara, than by what happens in Washington or Cleveland. I want the Africans to know that we Americans are interested in them as human beings, that we are there to help them as human beings, and that we would be there to help them if there were no communism in the world at all.

None of our doctors go overseas to wait upon the expatriate community, to hang around the local country club drinking warm beer. Our doctors are all assigned to indigenous medical institutions where they can give an example of what Toynbee called Western Man at his best. . . .

We have contacted some young American poets and have asked them to go to South America as faculty members at universities. We have asked poets to do this because many Latin Americans think of the United States as a place inhabited 100 per cent by businessmen working for Sears, Roebuck & Co., Socony Vacuum, Anaconda Copper and Pan American Grace, not to mention United Fruit.

In general, they have no idea that ordinary North Americans, gringos like you and me, are interested in music, or poetry, or art. These aspects of life are often more important to many South Americans than economic matters. But they think we are "Philistines" preoccupied only with money and profits. And the Communists encourage them to think so.

There is a newspaper published in Colombia for the *campesinos*—the small peasant farmers of that land—most of them uneducated, untraveled and, until recently, ignored.

Page one in the last two issues of this newspaper has been devoted to a poetry contest. Why to a poetry contest? There wasn't a word on page one about Wallace's hybrid corn, or Olin Mathieson's phosphate pill to increase food production. Probably there should have been, but instead there was a poetry contest. Can you imagine how successful a poetry magazine for Iowa farmers would be?

We've got to learn to communicate with people who prefer poetry to peanuts; otherwise we will never be able to reach inside of them and get them interested in food production, health, economic development, or any other of the subjects to which we attach so much importance.

Take another example: At Peace Corps headquarters we're now exploring the possibility of sending a jazz combo to a specific South American nation. Music is a language which opens many minds as well as many hearts. Jazz is popular, especially with the younger people in South America, and we have been lucky enough to find a group of brilliant young jazz musicians, all of them college graduates, three with M.A.'s, who have indicated that they are willing to give up their promising careers here in the United States to serve in the Peace Corps for two years, at $75 a month.

I think these young musicians may well be able to reach into the minds and hearts of young South Americans more effectively

than politicians. These musicians would not be wandering trou-
badours. They would have full-time jobs on a full-time music
faculty. Like all Peace Corps teaching personnel they would be
an integral part of a foreign academic community.

Poetry and music and the healing arts of medicine are not the
only languages we use. We are now exploring a project with
American schools of journalism whereby young Americans with
special gifts and training in the journalistic arts can become
teachers of these skills in universities around the world. Once
again we believe the language of journalism may be as effective
as formalized instruction in English grammar or literature. We
want classroom teachers of English literature. The world wants
them. But we also believe there are many ways to skin a cat—and
journalism may be one way in which to attract and instruct enter-
prising young people of foreign nations.

Science, too, has its language and we are fortunate at the Peace
Corps to have with us already overseas more than one hundred
young teachers of science who are using that language as a means
of communication between us Western men and the non-Western
majority of mankind in the world today.

You will note that the word "young" Americans slipped out
just then. There's no doubt that most of us in this room tonight
consider someone 25 years old to be young. That's our tough luck.
The 32-year-old minister of economic development for Tunisia,
however, does not share our feelings. Nor does the 34-year-old
foreign minister of the Congo, Justin Bomboko; or the 31-year-old
party leader in Kenya, Tom Mboya; or the 32-year-old secretary
general of the labor congress in Ghana, John Tettegah; or the
33-year-old prime minister and king of Morocco, Hassan II; or the
33-year-old prime minister of Tanganyika, Rashidi Kawawa.

Youth is not a liability for the Peace Corps or for our country.
It's a great asset. The Peace Corps is fortunate to have placed instructors of approximately 25 to 26 years of age on the faculties of
various universities around the world. We now have 10 teachers
on the faculty of Chulalongkorn University in Bangkok; 30 teachers on the faculty of the University of the East in Venezuela; and

soon we shall have 8 teachers at the University of Huamanga at Ayacucho in Peru; 20 additional teachers at the University of the East in Venezuela; 25 teachers at the University of Ife in Nigeria; 25 teachers at the University of the Philippines in Quezon City and Los Baños. . . .

And now for a few closing points.

1. The total number of people volunteering for the Peace Corps in February was the highest of any month in our history. More than three thousand new volunteers responded in February alone to the President's challenge: "Ask not what America will do for you, but what together we can do for the freedom of man."

2. The head of our Selection Division, Professor Lowell Kelly, Chairman of the Department of Psychology of the University of Michigan, has reported to me that the quality of the men and women volunteering for the Peace Corps today is as good, and in some cases, better than those who first responded to the President's call. We are in no danger of running out of qualified Americans of high character and ability to serve in the Peace Corps overseas.

3. Every state in the Union has already produced members of the Peace Corps. Every race in our country is represented—every creed. There has been no discrimination on the basis of race, color, or creed in the recruitment, the selection, the training or the assignment of Peace Corps volunteers.

4. Overseas, the Peace Corps volunteers have been received everywhere by the people of foreign lands and by government officials with enthusiasm, warmth and generosity. In Nigeria, where expatriate university teachers have been present in large numbers for over a quarter of a century, the government staged an official reception at the Federal Palace Hotel in Lagos when the first small Peace Corps contingent of thirty-five volunteers arrived, and more than one thousand civic leaders and government officials showed up to welcome this small but pioneering group.

In Ghana, the foreign minister, the minister of information, the minister of interior, and other cabinet members said of the Peace Corps: "That's one thing your country is doing properly."

In Colombia, the distinguished [former] president of that country, Alberto Lleras Camargo, said: "[The Peace Corps] is the finest way in which the United States could prove to the humble people of this and other lands that the primary purpose of its international aid program is to build a better life in all of the free world's villages and neighborhoods."

III. ACCOMPLISHMENTS

EDITOR'S INTRODUCTION

Teaching in Sierra Leone, Venezuela, and the Philippines; surveying roads and preparing geologic maps in Tanganyika; conducting community development projects in Colombia and Chile; working in health clinics in Malaya; carrying out agricultural extension and industrial education programs in India; and distributing books in the villages and schools of Pakistan— these are some of the many tasks of the approximately seven thousand Peace Corpsmen in some forty-five countries.

Beyond these facts and figures are the most important accomplishments. The volunteers live and work among the host country's people and have been able to develop a new image of the American citizen sharply different from that created by the isolated communities of American military officers, career diplomats, and corporation representatives. In turn, the Peace Corpsmen have acquired an appreciation of other countries' customs, institutions, and problems, and it is expected that they will return to America with a better understanding of world affairs. They will bring this background to positions in government, foreign service, education, and business. Another achievement of this people-to-people program has been to demonstrate the ways of democracy and industrialization to people who have never been able to examine these institutions closely. For in the past large-scale military and technical assistance programs have not always directly affected large segments of foreign populations and have not always won friends among them.

Perhaps the most significant accomplishment of the Peace Corps has been to afford the opportunity to those who long for peace and understanding between peoples to carry out their ideals in action. It has given them a chance to contribute to the improvement of conditions in other countries. And it has offered their example to people throughout the world.

The record of the corps is illustrated in this section by the story of community development in a Latin American state as related by Ambassador Fulton Freeman; the views of Harris L. Wofford, Jr. (appointed a Peace Corps associate director in March 1964), when he served as a corps administrator in African nations, and the experiences of volunteers in Latin American, Asian, and African countries. The section ends with over-all summaries of achievements by the late President Kennedy and R. Sargent Shriver, Jr.

COMMUNITY DEVELOPMENT IN COLOMBIA [1]

When in May 1961, I was named U.S. ambassador to Colombia, one of my initial preoccupations was the knowledge that Colombia would be the first country in Latin America . . . to receive in contingent of Peace Corps volunteers. . . .

In a real sense the idea which eventually developed into this first South American Peace Corps program was initiated in 1958. In that year the Colombian Congress passed a law directing that the government encourage self-help community projects as a method to improve living conditions. The groundwork for President Kennedy's still unconceived program was further advanced in 1959 when President Alberto Lleras Camargo issued a decree creating a Division of Community Development (División de Acción Comunal), as an agency functioning under the Ministry of Government, and instructed all government agencies to co-operate. Out of the interest and activity created by this decree. CARE in collaboration with the National Federation of Coffee Growers undertook a survey of community development possibilities in Colombia. It was this survey that formed the basis on which CARE submitted its proposal for a rural community development program to the embryonic Peace Corps. . . . This proposal was accepted and a cost reimbursable contract was

[1] From "The Peace Corps-CARE—Experiment in Community Development in Colombia," article by Fulton Freeman, United States ambassador to Colombia (1961-64), and to Mexico (appointed in 1964). In *To Amend the Peace Corps Act;* hearings, October 15-16, 1963, on H.R. 8754. United States. Congress. House of Representatives. Committee on Foreign Affairs. 88th Congress, 1st session. The Committee. Washington, D.C. 20025. '63. p 60-7.

signed empowering CARE to develop and administer the program in cooperation with the Colombian government. In this contract CARE agreed to provide a minimum of $100,000 in program materials and equipment.

Throughout the months of June, July, and August of 1961, while Peace Corps and CARE officials were struggling with the problems of mounting the first training program, the CARE field operation was busy negotiating an agreement with the Colombian government to provide the framework of the present rural community development program. The resulting agreement has since been extended to include the urban community development program recently inaugurated by the Peace Corps in the larger cities of Colombia. This agreement sets forth the Colombian government's desire to have the volunteers work in Colombia in programs of rural community development; recognizes CARE as the administrating agency under authority granted by the agreement between the U.S. Peace Corps and the voluntary organization; establishes the term of the agreement and methods of its extension; names the Division of Community Development as the Colombian agency having the over-all responsibility for the program; creates a coordinating committee composed of one representative each from the division of Acción Comunal, the National Planning Board, CARE and the U.S. Embassy charged with the responsibility of over-all program direction with the power to extend or terminate the program as deemed appropriate; grants to CARE free importation privileges for the elements essential for the proper functioning of the program; and recognizes the Peace Corps-CARE operation as a separate technical mission from the existing operations of the CARE mission. This agreement was duly submitted to the U.S. Embassy in Bogotá for approval, completing all the necessary legal prerequisites, at the end of August 1961.

As of January 1963 there are three Peace Corps units operating under CARE administration in Colombia—two in rural community development and one in urban community development programs. The first unit arrived in September 1961, the second in May 1962, and the urban unit became operational in November 1962. . . .

One of the basic principles of the program has been that this Peace Corps effort should form an integral part of a Colombian program. In no sense should it be a self-contained effort imposed upon the Colombian scene and lacking direct, intimate relationship with the Colombian machinery established to create a national community development program. The concept of what constitutes community development in Colombia, therefore, has come from a meeting of minds between the program's administrators and the division of Acción Comunal of the Colombian government.

Community development is envisioned as a process whereby individuals at the grass-roots level learn to become alert, responsible citizens with the ability and the desire to enter into the decisions that will affect their future and the future of their families. . . . While tangible, physical works are an important tool in the development of a community, they are not the end for which the program is striving. The goal rather is an informed local citizenry that understands democracy at the grass-roots level and is making it work. It is to create . . . [in the villages and towns] active communities of interrelated human beings who have a sense of responsibility for one another and for their communal progress, and who realize that through democratic processes they can best attain the self-respect and the control of the destiny they desire and deserve. . . .

This is the context in which the Peace Corps volunteers are working in Colombia. It is probably too early to make definite conclusions and evaluations in a program of this type, but there are enough accomplishments and indications to allow one to form some fairly conclusive ideas as to the value of the volunteers' work and of the program itself. The following is a breakdown of Peace Corps-CARE program activities as of the end of 1962 involving 100 volunteers and 50 rural sites:

Schools: Built or extensively repaired, 16; in progress (including school kitchens, 98.

Roads: Built, 14; improved, 2; in progress, 46.
Bridges: Built, 6; in progress, 8.
Aqueducts: Built, 13; in progress, 29.
Health centers: Built, 2; in progress, 13.
Parks and plazas: Built, 1; in progress, 5.
Bazaars: In all sites.
English classes: In 13 sites.
Literacy classes: In 4 sites.
Sports programs: In 28 sites.
Latrine programs: In 16 sites.
School lunch programs: In 4 sites.
Electrification projects: 21 in progress.
Health education programs: In 10 sites.
Village industry and cooperatives: 19 programs in 16 sites.
Home construction or improvement projects: In 15 sites.
Agricultural improvement and reforestation programs: In 27 sites.
Miscellaneous:
    Film programs: In all sites.
    Small work projects, including street, path, and stream clear-
        ing; building drain ditches; repairing aqueducts, roads, and
        churches: In 12 sites.
    Community salon, center or kiosks constructed for community
        or club meetings: In 8 sites.
    Community development seminars held: In 8 sites.
    School or community libraries begun: In 8 sites.
    Pumps, wells, tanks installed: In 4 sites.
    Community census taken: In 3 sites.
    Cemetery walls built: In 2 sites.
    Weekly radio program on community development: In 1
        site.

While this list of tangible works is impressive, particularly
when it is realized that the program is little more than one year
old, an even more important accomplishment is the several
hundred local community organizations, with the associated
parent-teachers', boys' and girls', agricultural, and other allied
groups, which have been organized or revitalized by the Colom-

bian local promoters and their coworkers, the Peace Corps volunteers. To suggest that these organizations are all well-functioning democratic bodies effectively doing their job would indeed be misleading and an exaggeration. In fact, a majority of them probably are not, but the important thing is that they are in some stage of organization and that there is a definite program at the local level to try to improve this organization. The Colombian experience has shown that a great deal of activity in physical projects in a given community does not necessarily mean that the area is one in which there is a good community spirit and where local citizenry is learning to take its rightful and active part in its own affairs. The fact that some of these areas of high activity have resulted from a fortuitous circumstance of available outside aid coupled with a passive community—in other words, a community that will do as it's told by its recognized leaders. There is no actual participation, but simply the carrying out of orders. The works performed obviously result in advantages to the community, but the successful physical completions have not in some cases altered the existing social structures of the village as a passive, nonparticipating society responding to a paternalistic approach. Since a principal objective of the Peace Corps is to inspire local communities to do things for themselves, the volunteers strive to convert this nonparticipating attitude wherever they find it to an imaginative and constructive one.

Normally, of course, a successful physical project is essential to get the process of a community development started in a given area. And conversely, a failure to successfully complete a project once undertaken does deep harm to any community development effort. This is especially true if aid definitely promised, particularly from the government itself, is not forthcoming when the community has completed its part of the project. Unfortunately, this all too often has been the case in the first year of the program's operation in Colombia. This lack of outside assistance to the community efforts being put forth under the community development program has been the one most recurrent problem that has confronted the Peace Corps volunteers and their coworkers. This outside aid, particularly governmental, forms an essential part of any local community's efforts to improve itself. This is especially true in a country where the standard of living and earning capacity at the lower economic levels are so limited. Not only is this outside help necessary to complete needed community projects, but it is also necessary to demonstrate to the community that its government and other outside agencies are interested and willing to join with the community in a united effort to improve its lot in life. The failure to provide needed outside assistance is not simply a matter of money, surprisingly enough, but in a large measure a problem of public administration and education of public functionaries at all levels. It has been shown time after time in the program that, given the desire and the knowledge of how to get things done within the Colombian governmental structure on the part of public officials, the necessary aid is forthcoming.

A well-organized, functioning community development program resulting in changes in the thinking patterns and living habits of the people is not something that happens overnight. Nor is it something that can be successfully implanted by foreigners. Every community development program must be tailored to the local cultural and habit patterns and it must be planned in such a way as to give continuity to its efforts so that its beneficial effects will become lasting threads in the national fabric. The Peace Corps community development program has, therefore, from the beginning put great importance upon the counterpart idea and upon the necessity of fitting the work of the volunteers into the framework of Colombian efforts instead of creating an isolated and unrelated program. The volunteers became workers within an existing Colombian structure, even though this structure prior to the arrival of the volunteers was barely in the formative stage. Each team of two volunteers works with a Colombian counterpart called a *promotor local* (local promoter or village worker). This counterpart may be an employee of one of several organizations—The National Division of Community Development, one of the seventeen provinces, the Federation of Coffee Growers, or in a few cases a municipality. Generally, these promoters are grammar school graduates who have completed a six-month special course in community development given by the Division of Community Development. Some of the promoters, however have received their *bachillerato,* which is roughly equivalent to the U.S. high school diploma. These workers . . . are trained strictly as village organizers whose job it is to act as catalysts and educators to the village to help it channel its energies in the most efficient manner. Ideally the village-level worker and his Peace Corps helpers have a polyvalent team on which to call for technical services. This team is made up of a doctor and/or nurse, an agricultural specialist and a home visitor. Unfortunately only in the coffee zones is this the case, rarely in the noncoffee areas. With more adequate financing, however, this is what the division plans to have in each municipality in which community development work is being carried on.

Given the vast differences in cultural and educational backgrounds between the Colombian promoters and the Peace Corps volunteers, one might expect that there would be a great deal of friction. This would seem to be more the case when it is realized that the volunteers are supposed to take a subservient role in the team and that the Colombian promoter is considered the leader. It is a lot to ask of the highly motivated, dynamic volunteer, who knows he has but two short years to accomplish something lasting and satisfying, that he accept a secondary role from someone who is his educational inferior and frequently has no more experience in the work than the volunteer himself. It is a testament both to the volunteer's selfless spirit and dedication to the program's goals, on the one hand, and to the innate intelligence, sensitiveness, and inborn courtesy of the Colombian coworker on the other, that this counterpart relationship has gone as well as it has. This is not to stay that all teams have functioned well and that there have not been frictions. Most certainly there have, but none has been so serious as adversely to affect the program. There has been a healthy spirit of give and take on both sides that has enabled the Peace Corps volunteers and the counterparts to grow in their jobs and to learn from each other to the advantage of the whole effort. In some cases very close personal attachments have occurred. The more common occurrence, however, is the development of a working arrangement based on sincere mutual respect. Each has come to realize that he needs the other and that the program needs them both.

At the outset the volunteers had trouble getting their counterparts to take the initiative and fulfill their role as leader of the team. Of late this has been changing, and as the counterparts gain experience and confidence they are assuming the leadership, in some instances even more vigorously than the volunteers feel is required. It is of course far better that the counterpart tend toward too much responsibility for the work rather than too little, and it is just the volunteers' lot to have to live with this fact.

One aspect of the program that has fulfilled the fondest hopes of even the most optimistic has been the acceptance of the Peace Corps volunteers by Colombians at all social levels. The manner in which the volunteers have adapted to the rigorous living conditions and to cultural patterns so different from their own should be a source of pride to all Americans, and should reinforce our faith in the American way of life that has produced these volunteers. The affection and respect that is felt for the volunteers by the Colombian villagers is a palpable thing that can be noted even by the most casual observer visiting the villages. Tearful farewells are commonplace when volunteers are transferred. Such evidences of village acceptance as naming volunteers as *padrines* or godparents and the granting of special gifts and proclamations have been numerous. Almost without exception, the transfer of a Peace Corps volunteer for administrative reasons or the closing of a site due to lack of proper progress has brought forth letters of protest and visits of commissions from the village to Bogotá. . . .

Due to the wide dispersion of the Peace Corps volunteers, the difficult communications, and the rigid structuring on the part of the Colombian agencies with which the volunteers work, the administrational and operational aspects of the program have proved complicated and difficult. Since these initial difficulties appear to have been surmounted successfully, it might be worth while to examine, superficially at least, the manner in which this program is administered.

The Peace Corps has established an office in Colombia staffed by a Peace Corps country director and, at the present time, two deputies. The director is responsible for keeping the ambassador and Washington informed regarding the various Peace Corps programs in the country and has responsibility for the proper over-all functioning of the various Peace Corps programs. He maintains contact with Colombian government officials of all levels with regard to the existing programs and in the developing of future Peace Corps activities. Not all future programs will be under CARE-Peace Corps. Some will be under other private agencies; some will be administered directly by the Peace Corps itself. In the community development program close liaison is maintained between the Peace Corps director's office and the office of the operating agency, CARE-Peace Corps.

CARE-Peace Corps is presently administered by a project director and four associate project directors. Those personnel serve both the urban and rural programs. The general responsibilities are divided into two fields. The first is programing and pertains to all aspects of program development and material support, and the second is the personnel and logistical phase of the program. An associate project director is assigned one of these responsibilities and answers to the director. The director on his part is the responsible officer to the Peace Corps as well as to the Colombian government for carrying out the terms of the various agreements. Serving as field supervisors are ten Peace Corps volunteer leaders. These leaders are provided wth jeeps and are assigned certain geographical zones. They are constantly on the move among the various sites in their zones and report weekly to the Bogotá office regarding the general state of the programs in the sites visited, the health and welfare of the volunteers, and the relationships between the volunteers and the Colombian agencies. They also serve as expediters of material support, particularly that coming from the CARE organization and directly from the Peace Corps. Individual volunteers are required on their part to file monthly reports on activities as well as a report on sick, vacation, and rest days taken throughout the month.

The Peace Corps and CARE-Peace Corps staff members maintain a rigorous visitation schedule and attempt to visit each site at least once every three months. . . .

Generalities on a program of this nature cannot give the reader a very clear conception of the day-to-day work of the individual volunteers. In an effort to provide some of the flavor of these varied activities, there follow summaries of recent monthly reports from volunteers. . . .

Report covering the period October 15 to November 15 [1962], site of Manaure in the Department of Magdalena. This is an isolated village situated on the boundary between Magdalena and the territory of La Guajira in the extreme north of Colombia. It is a coffee-growing area and the volunteers work with the Coffee Extension Team and have a counterpart local community developer provided by the Departmental Committee of Coffee Growers. The volunteers reported nine community meetings attended, with fifteen community workdays held with an average attendance of five villagers per workday. They also reported that during the subject period a new project of fund raising for the Health Center of Manaure had been started and that projects in process during the period were the building of a school and a carpentry shop in one of the *veredas* [roadside settlements] of the municipality, rabbit hutch and bee-raising projects, and development work for an electrification project in which the generator is to be provided from AID [U.S. Agency for International Development]. During this same period they completed one rabbit hutch project and finished construction on a school up to the point of being ready to raise the roof. They reported that they had received support and cooperation from the coffee committee in the way of materials for the school, received an approval from CARE to provide a rotary saw for the installation of a small sawmill, and received tools to be used in the school construction and local 4-S projects (4-S are similar to the 4-H Clubs in the United States). They stated their most acute problem at present is the delay in the arrival of the generator coming through AID, since the community had moved much faster than was expected. They completed the report stating that the work plans for the following month would include primarily the pushing of the rabbit and bee projects with 4-S clubs, since it is coffee harvest and the farmers are all extremely busy and will not be available for much community work. . . .

Moving to the extreme south of the country, the volunteers working in Gigante, Huila, reported that ten community meetings were attended during the month and that eight community workdays were held with an average attendance of twenty to twenty-five people per workday. During the month three new organizations were established, all of them veredal construction committees to assist in the construction work in their areas. During the reporting period an all-day fiesta was held to celebrate the beginning of the school construction and the closing of the old school, with such projects in process as the building of a stand where the local 4-S Clubs can sell soft drinks and food and the working on an aqueduct. . . . Such support and cooperation received were reported as the provision of a foreman to direct the construction of the school and the supplying of pipe for the school aqueduct, all coming from the coffee growers' committee. Good cooperation was also reported from the mayor of Gigante who arranged for the use of the municipal truck to transport bricks to the school worksite. Volunteer plans for the ensuing period called for pushing construction on the school, finishing the 4-S stand, and organizing an all-day fiesta with two of the *veredas* to raise money for their work projects. Volunteers requested help to interest the public health officials in the construction of a health center for the area. . . .

Even from this small sampling, the great diversity of activities in which the volunteers are involved can be appreciated. What is less apparent, however, is the disproportionate amount of time spent in traveling many miles by horseback or afoot to far-off sections of their municipalities to attend meetings or to assist local groups in activating community organizations. A great deal more of their time is spent in simply waiting for people to arrive for a given meeting and in house-to-house visits to explain, to cajole, to inspire, or to just inform the people. They must work with all sectors of the community from the youngsters to the town elders and must make every effort to establish cordial working relationships with the priests, the traditional village leaders, and politicians, as well as with the new generation of leaders, who are rising to the surface with the development and the proper functioning of democratic community organizations.

It can be said without exaggeration that no other U.S. Government program has so completely captured the imagination of the *campesinos* of Colombia as has the Peace Corps program. The fact that they have living in their village one or two young Americans, stoically accepting the same physical discomforts and the same dietary restrictions, who work with them day after day, getting to know their homes, their problems, their farms, and their hills, as integral members of the community, has made a lasting impact on these people. It has also made it possible for a deep comprehension to develop between the American and the Colombian. . . .

As I suggested at the outset, it is probably too early to arrive at a definitive evaluation of the Peace Corps-CARE program in Colombia, and it would certainly be premature to pass judgment on the permanence of the gradual changes which are being observed in the villages where volunteers are stationed. It cannot be gainsaid, however, that an important beginning has been made in the establishment of a national community development program in Colombia which may well have a profound effect on the pace and nature of Colombia's social and economic development in conjunction with the Alliance for Progress. It has also been conclusively demonstrated that our young American Peace Corps volunteers have the necessary ability, imagination, courage, and, most importantly, empathy to accept with grace the same living and working conditions which are standard for their local coworkers in woefully underdeveloped, rural areas while succeeding as effective good-will ambassadors and realizing solid accomplishments in community development.

PIONEERS [2]

REPRINTED BY PERMISSION; © 1962 THE NEW YORKER MAGAZINE, INC.

Last week, we accompanied Harris L. Wofford, Jr., Special Representative for the Peace Corps for Africa, as he drove seventy-five miles upstate to greet five dozen freshly recruited volunteers for the Teachers for Sierra Leone Peace Corps Project. Mr. Wofford had just resigned as Special Assistant to President Kennedy on the Peace Corps and on Civil Rights in order to assume his new job. The training site, and our destination, was the State University College, in New Paltz. Mr. Wofford, driving a rented car and accompanied by a young diplomat named J. C. W. Porter, who is Third Secretary to the Sierra Leone Embassy, in Washington, picked us up, by prearrangement, in front of the new local Peace Corps office, a store front on East Forty-second Street that is staffed by attractive, steady-eyed young people and festooned with decorative brochures ("TEACHERS in the Peace Corps," "WOMEN in the Peace Corps," "AMERICAN LABOR in the Peace Corps," "HEALTH PROFESSIONS in the Peace Corps," "YOU and the Peace Corps"). We got into the front seat with Mr. Wofford. Mr. Porter told us he had some papers he'd like to spread out in the rear, and after Wofford had dutifully pointed out a traffic jam, an Automat, the United Nations headquarters, and the Triborough Bridge, Porter said he was going to work on his notes for a speech he was scheduled to make to the recruits.

Wofford, a tall, broad-shouldered man of thirty-six, with a ringing voice and a kind of All-America handsomeness, told us that in August he plans to move from Chevy Chase to Addis Ababa, with his wife, Clare, and their three children—Susanne, Daniel, and David, who are ten, seven, and two. "The greatest future of the Peace Corps is in Africa," he said. "I've been to Africa four times this past year. Each time I got there, I felt myself going into high gear. I had the feeling of being in tune with the world. In my new job, I'll be administrator of the Ethiopian program as well as the representative for our work in all the other

[2] Article in *New Yorker*. 38:24-7. Je. 30, '62. Reprinted by permission.

African nations. I'm campaigning to recruit three hundred teachers for the secondary schools of Ethiopia—that's about as many teachers as they've got now. The population of the country is twenty million. Almost a million Ethiopian children should be in academic secondary schools, but only six thousand are. The population of Sierra Leone is two and a half million, and no more than seven thousand children attend the equivalent of high school. The Peace Corps sent about forty teachers over there six months ago, and of this new batch that we're going to see now we hope to send forty or fifty more. The Peace Corps is only a year old, and we've got a thousand volunteers working now, in fourteen countries all over the world—minimum age, eighteen; maximum age, unlimited. We'll have two thousand, in twenty-seven countries, by September, and five thousand by 1963. The Peace Corps is the main embodiment of the New Frontier. President Kennedy says that the Peace Corps is going to restore the American spirit. I happen to feel that the Peace Corps is awakening our slumbering pioneering traditions. As a lawyer, I know that lawyers are all frustrated founding fathers. Lawyers would like to have been around when our Constitution was written. They would like to have chartered all the basic institutions of the country. Well, we've just launched a program to recruit lawyers into the Peace Corps. We've got forty law schools in the country lined up to coöperate with us. We'll give the lawyers a chance to work as clerks in Ministries and in the African courts, to assist in drafting codes, and to teach in the new law schools. But law is just one part of what the Peace Corps can help create in Africa. It's all so wide open. And limited only by our imagination. It's an empty continent. In Asia or in Latin America, the poverty, in a way, closes in on you. But in Africa you can drive fifty miles and not see anybody. You get a feeling there that must be like what the people felt who first saw America. Africans are a young people, making history. They're starting out with a clean slate and writing on it what they want to write. Their No. 1 investment is in education. We in the Peace Corps want to encourage the African countries to think even bigger than they've been thinking so far in terms of moving ahead. By doubling the secondary-school populations this year, we'll develop hundreds of college graduates qualified to teach school in Africa, and we'll really be on our way."

A light glinted in Wofford's eyes. Glancing behind us, we saw Porter completely absorbed in his notes. "Why Africa for *you?*" we asked Wofford. "Why not stick around in Washington, and go to a few parties?"

"White House social life has added a certain lustre to social life around the country, a certain radiance," Wofford said. "But I believe in forming the world you want to create as well as you can with what's within your reach—a political clue I learned from Gandhi. My whole life so far has been a rhythm between the race question in the world and the race question at home. I call one the big integration and the other the little integration. During the Presidential campaign, I helped draft the civil-rights section of the Democratic platform. I kind of resisted the Peace Corps for a long time, because I felt I ought to try to do something that was not so natural for me. But I couldn't hold out any longer. In my letter of resignation, I told the President that it was time, I felt, to work not from a desk in Washington but from where I want to live, in Africa, where I'll be constantly on the scene. He wrote back with complete understanding and warm good wishes."

"Well," we said, "how did all this start? Where were you born?"

"In New York City, on April 9, 1926," Wofford said. "I grew up in Johnson City, Tennessee, and in Scarsdale. My maternal grandmother came from Little Rock. We were very close. When I was eleven—the last year I was eligible to travel at half fare—she took me out of school for seven months, which we spent travelling around the world on tramp steamers. I saw sixteen countries. In Rome, I heard Mussolini roar from his balcony the night he cancelled Italy's membership in the League of Nations. In India, I saw the poverty of Bombay and Calcutta. After Pearl Harbor, while I was at Scarsdale High School, Clarence Streit's

idea for the Atlantic Community took hold of me, and in the
name of the Federalists, who transformed the alliance of the thir-
teen American colonies into a true federation, I founded the Student Federalists. I was its first national president. My wife, by
the way, was its third national president. We met at the first national convention. I graduated from high school in 1944 and
spent twenty months as an Air Force trainee at Craig Field, Alabama, after which I attended the University of Chicago, graduat-
ing in 1948. Then I got married, went to India and Pakistan with
my wife for seven months, came home, and wrote a book with
her called 'India Afire.' After that, we wanted to go to Israel, and
we did. We worked on a *kibbutz* and looked over the country
quite thoroughly. When we got home, I decided to study law at
Howard University. It was 1950, a very creative period in civil-
rights law, and the center of all the litigation was at Howard.
Also, I'd never been in a position to know many Negroes, and the
chance to be a fellow-student of Negroes appealed to me very
much. I didn't think it would hurt me to be a member of a
minority for a while. After getting full law degrees from both
Howard and Yale, I became a special assistant to Chester Bowles.
I also practiced law in Washington pretty regularly, until 1958,
with the firm of Covington & Burling. In 1959, I joined the
faculty of Notre Dame Law School and taught for a year; I have
been away on a leave of absence ever since. The things that interest me are everywhere."

Arriving in New Paltz, we drew up before a brick dormitory
building assigned to Peace Corps trainees, and Wofford said, "Mr.
Porter, do you have your speech?"

"I will thank the volunteers for leaving all comforts here to go
to Sierra Leone," Porter said, "and warn them that the first few
months they may be treated with indifference, but the indifference
will go away when they show they came to help, not to dominate.
I will say, 'Go there with an open heart and do a good job.'"

To the strains of "Home, Sweet Home" piped haltingly on
a recorder by some invisible trainee, we went inside, and there
we were immediately enveloped by a throng of very young-look-

ing trainees: "I'm Rufus Stevenson, Newman, Georgia, which I left at 6 A.M. this morning." "I'm Judy Salisbury, Westfield, New Jersey, and I'm rather surprised to be going to Sierra Leone." "I'm Thomas Birnberg, Los Angeles, California." "I'm Bill Whitten, Milwaukee, Wisconsin." "I'm Bob Gross, New York City." "I'm Bill Prosch, Birmingham, Alabama." "I'm Bill Graham, Falls Church, Virginia. I'm going to teach history. How can those Africans have a sense of their world without history?" "I'm Bruce Pearson, Greenwich, Connecticut."

Then we met some Peace Corps administrators: "I'm Dr. Joseph Murphy, and I teach political philosophy at Brandeis University. I decided to spend my summer working for the Peace Corps. One thing that anybody from the academic world finds when he associates himself with the Peace Corps is that the volunteers have more resourcefulness, more intelligence, more energy, more enthusiasm, more of everything than you'll ever see in the average undergraduate." "I'm George Goba. I teach Mende, the main language of the biggest tribe in Sierra Leone. I come from Taiama, a town of three thousand in Sierra Leone. Taiama has the best bridge in the country. I am so *proud* of that bridge. My mother still lives in Taiama, and many of my friends. They write that a Peace Corps girl came to Taiama, and they asked her to show them how to do the Twist, and she did not know, and they laughed and laughed at her ignorance. I wrote to my friends and said I had met some Americans here who asked me to show them how to do the High Life, the popular African dance, and I did not know, and they laughed and laughed at my ignorance. I left Taiama six years ago, when I was twenty-three, and I hope to go back when I become a doctor. I am studying medicine at Fairleigh Dickinson University. I used to be a houseboy for missionaries in Taiama, and when my father died, they helped me come to America to study. My sister Nancy, who is twenty-one, has just come to America. She is in the state of Indiana studying to become a nurse." "I am Dr. David Crabb. I was born in Newark, New Jersey. I am an anthropological linguist. I teach Swahili. Anybody can speak Swahili. There's nothing to it."

And, finally, we attended a dinner in honor of the trainees and listened to the official welcoming speech, given by Wofford: "Everywhere you go in the world you meet American education coming back. . . . In a very real sense, we are going to learn as much as we teach . . . to see whether we of the West, the true minority of the world, can become integrated with the new world, whether we can join the human race. . . . The New Frontiers are not in Washington. . . . They are out where you are going. . . ."

SEÑOR RON [3]

Ronald C. Atwater is a twenty-four-year-old MIT graduate who is blessed with the outgoing friendliness of a puppy, the brass of a door-to-door salesman, and the ingenuity of an old-fashioned Yankee tinkerer. But on his first assignment, organizing community projects in the village of Guachetá [Colombia], about fifty miles north of Bogotá, he found that he couldn't fight city hall.

Atwater's engaging smile, ruffled copper-red hair, and fondness for *campesino* [country-style] clothes won over the townspeople. Yet when he tried to put up a school, the mayor insisted it be built on an expensive lot owned by a friend. And when Atwater suggested building a road to serve the *campesinos* in the hills, the mayor swung it around to reach the big landowners' homes in the valley.

One day last fall [1962], Atwater decided he had outlived his usefulness in Guachetá. He saddled up his horse, loaded a borrowed burro with three dozen paperbacks, a Remington portable typewriter, his machete, guitar, half a case of beer, and a supply of Spam provided by the United States Embassy, and headed south.

New Home

Ten miles back in the mountains, Atwater found Lengua-zaque, a misty village of 600 souls perched at 9,600 feet, where

[3] From article by Milan J. Kubic, chief Latin American correspondent, *Newsweek*. *Newsweek*. 61:48. Je. 3, '63. Reprinted by permission.

the temperature is always in the 40's and it rains almost every day. Together with a new Peace Corps partner, John P. Schaubel, and with Raúl Hincapié, their Colombian counterpart, Atwater rented a primitive house for $8 a month and set up housekeeping, camping-style.

This time, local authorities supported the Peace Corps team. Atwater helped found the community's first newspaper, a mimeographed weekly. He also organized the construction of five schools and planned for a community center.

Still he wasn't satisfied. Next to potatoes, the town's chief product was *ruanas*, hand-woven ponchos. But the weavers were barely eking out a living from the few *ruanas* they managed to peddle on the streets of Bogotá, four hours away by train.

Atwater went from door to door, inviting the weavers to a meeting in the town hall. "Let me help you form a marketing cooperative," he confidently suggested. "I'll guarantee you a better demand and higher prices." The suspicious weavers, Atwater recalled, "just about told me to go to hell."

Undeterred, Atwater donned his Sunday suit and went off to Bogotá to visit a dye factory. There he picked up a bunch of free dye samples and a promise of a 45 per cent discount on future purchases, and talked the manager into teaching him the technique of dyeing wool. Back in Lenguazaque, he passed out the samples and persuaded two weavers to let him try to sell their best *ruanas*. Once again in city clothes, Atwater made the rounds of Bogotá's best souvenir shops offering "a steady supply of guaranteed quality *ruanas* at a guaranteed price." When he returned to Lenguazaque displaying a fistful of orders, he was welcomed with *abrazos* [embraces].

Booming Trade

Atwater taught the weavers to dye wool properly and to improve quality and design. Sixteen weavers now supply him with *ruanas,* and he hopes to bring all twenty-five into the cooperative. Every Thursday he rises at 4 A.M. to catch the bus to Bogotá to deliver the $9 *ruanas* which are then retailed for $16. He also exports them to the States. His advertising flyer brazenly plugging handmade Colombian *ruanas* as a Peace Corps project brought two hundred orders from stores from Boston to Los Angeles. Atwater's salesmanship has doubled the weavers' incomes.

The *ruana* business has had its rough moments. Atwater once loaned one young weaver $25; the man promptly disappeared with a girl. Feeling somewhat responsible, Atwater stretched his tiny Peace Corps living allowance to help support the weaver's wife and three children. Three weeks later, the husband sheepishly came back, broke. On another occasion, Atwater ran afoul of Peace Corps brass: a Bogotá staff director threatened to send him back to the United States for appearing in the capital "uncombed, unwashed, unshaven, with mud on his shoes." Big landowners in the neighborhood labeled him a "Yankee exploiter" and then a "Communist." But the townspeople feel differently. "We all love Señor Ron," said one man. "He is a good Yankee."

Señor Ron intends to stay on in Lenguazaque until September, when he hopes his cooperative will be formally established and bursting with fall orders from the United States. "First I'll head for California," he said, "and take an M.A. in business administration. Then I'll come back to South America—working, I hope, for a private firm."

Sitting in his dingy "office" last week, the ebullient Atwater looked out the window at the rain clouds and pondered a few questions about the Peace Corps. "I guess we help," he said, grinning. "I know I'm having a ball. This is the best time of my life."

PEACE CORPS COUPLE TYPIFY NEW TREND [4]

Last fall, chemical engineer Carl Gibson and his wife Jane, a chemist, left for Uttar Pradesh Agricultural University at Pant-

[4] Reprinted from *Chemical and Engineering News*, Vol. 41, No. 7, February 18, 1963, pages 92-4. Copyright 1963 by the American Chemical Society and reprinted by permission of the copyright owner.

nagar, India. They are there as part of a fifty-member contingent to help expand and teach the school's science curriculum, as well as to do research and agricultural extension work. The Gibsons are Peace Corps volunteers.

They represent a new trend in Peace Corps volunteers—a trend toward more highly skilled technical manpower. "We would like to have at least 10 per cent of our manpower scientifically oriented," Jules Pagano, director of the Peace Corps professional and technical division, says. "The problems facing developing nations call for above-average volunteers," he adds.

The Gibsons are certainly that. Carl, twenty-eight, is from Middleton, Wisconsin. He received his B.S. and M.S. in chemical engineering from the University of Wisconsin and his Ph.D. from Stanford. Jane, who is twenty-six, hails from Paris, Texas. She completed her undergraduate work in chemistry at the University of Tennessee before moving on to Stanford for her master's degree in physical sciences.

Although volunteers are encouraged to choose a country that especially interests them, the Gibsons did not. They were assigned to India because of that country's critical need for university science teachers and for help in modernizing its agriculture. . . .

In India, the Gibsons have a varied work schedule. During school months, both teach chemistry at the university. Carl also conducts some graduate work, and his wife assists.

After school, they help with community development activities. Helping to bridge social distances found in highly stratified societies is one of their most important functions.

When school is out this spring, the Gibsons will work informally with their students, leading discussion groups and taking them on field trips. And they will do research on specific problems of the area, such as farming techniques, soil conservation, and nourishment.

"In this capacity we have found people like the Gibsons to be of far greater benefit than just teachers or farmers because they have the ability to relate classroom theory to the real problems of the country," says Mr. Pagano.

Americans of all ages and backgrounds are responding to the Peace Corps call for volunteers. The Indian contingent, for example, includes the Gibsons, a nineteen-year-old boy with two years of college who is teaching livestock improvement, and a woman, sixty-nine, who formerly taught English in South Dakota. . . .

Jane sums up what motivated her and her husband: "We would like to be in a position to let people know what Americans are like by being a good example. We will try to win friends for ourselves and for our country. Maybe these efforts will mean that the next generation won't be going to the same countries to kill." A willingness to serve and a useful skill are the two most essential qualifications for Peace Corps service, Mr. Pagano says.

Training for the Future

What does the future hold for the volunteer when he returns from abroad? "We've established a division of volunteer field support to deal with the personal problems of the volunteer," Mr. Pagano explains. "It gets information to him on what is happening while he is away and what will be available to him on his return."

According to Mr. Pagano, many schools and industries, as well as Federal agencies, already have expressed interest in interviewing returning volunteers. "Volunteer files will be available to these people," he says, "so they can see the record of achievement—the kind of reaction a volunteer received from other countries and the people he worked with."

For returning volunteers who have not finished their education and would like to, the Peace Corps, working with a number of colleges and universities, is exploring the possibilities of giving some form of academic credit for Peace Corps service. Then, too, the $1,800 severance pay will be a big help to those who had to curtail education for lack of money.

Some companies have expanded their military or government leave policies to include employees who join the Peace Corps.

This ensures the volunteer that his job will be waiting for him when he returns.

But the Peace Corps is limited in what it can do to further the careers of its returnees. "Congress has specifically forbidden us to be an employment agency in any sense," Mr. Pagano stresses. "We can't give people special treatment just because they are in the Peace Corps.". . .

As the Peace Corps enters its second year of operation even some of its most vociferous early opponents now admit that it is a surprising success. Since its first mission of fifty-one to Ghana in 1961, the Peace Corps has grown until today there are more than five thousand volunteers serving in forty countries. In his State of the Union Message [1963], President Kennedy predicted that by 1964 more than nine thousand volunteers will be serving overseas.

Even now, demand for . . . [volunteers] is so great that no country has received the number it has requested, Mr. Pagano says. This is particularly true of secondary-school science teachers. "More and more countries are asking for volunteers trained in science and technology," he says. "The success of our future projects to a large extent hinges strongly on the cooperation and support of the scientific community."

"YOU JUST PLUNGE IN" [5]

My introduction to public-health nursing in Sokodé, Togo, was the Polyclinique: an amorphous, sighing building of a diaper-yellow color, bulging with soft women in brightly hued clothes walking over each other to be first to the consultation room, . . . children in khaki school uniforms picking their sores and searching around for used bandages, and fat babies making puddles under the benches. I decided what I was going to bring to the Polyclinique was "organization."

[5] From article by Margaret Michelle McEvoy, nurse and member of Peace Corps medical team in Sokodé, Togo, West Africa. *Peace Corps Volunteer.* 2:6-8. February '64.

With flawless logic, wild gestures, stern stares, rope barriers, and a three-word Kotokoli vocabulary, I tried to teach these happy people the meaning of queues. They giggled.

In my second month in Sokodé, I was told I could run the school health program. There were schools—eight of them—little health, and no program.

School nursing: it is latrine-building, inoculation-giving, stool- and urine-collecting. It is also parent-cajoling, milk-mixing, film-projecting, and knowing how to change flat tires on a motorbike.

There is no formal starting place; you just plunge in. Rarely have the children been seen by a doctor. They have not been immunized. Since there are no latrines in the schools or in the town, infectious parasites are everywhere. . . .

[A church mission] was distributing large quantities of powdered milk to the schools. No one knew how to mix it, and the children either ate it in powdered form or rubbed it in their hair. Those who managed to get some home mixed it in polluted water, got sick, and gave milk a bad name in the community.

In our milk program we used the simplest implements imaginable: a twenty-liter bucket and clean hands. We taught first the teachers and then a team of older children how to mix the milk and distribute it. This time the project worked. The students adored the milk and we had to have "milk-mustache check" to see that some wouldn't come back for seconds before all had had firsts. . . .

When Dr. Nick Cunningham (Springfield Centre, N.Y.) and I first started doing physical examinations in the schools, we gave each child a questionnaire on his eating habits, his past illnesses, and what he thought was wrong with him. We got back compositions from the students telling us how their heads would mysteriously turn every time they had to open a schoolbook. Some of the responses were note-in-a-bottle messages like "Help help O you of the Health! They are giving us rotten water to drink! There are worms in the soup!" To the question "How many times a week do you eat meat?" the answer was invariably, *"Grand jamais!"*—a big NEVER. This year we decided that questionnaires invited too much creative writing, so we dropped the idea.

Anyway, we started off by examining twelve children per afternoon. There are 4,000 school children in Sokodé, and going at that rate we saw only 800. Under new procedures this year we are examining 100 children an afternoon and passing 250 children a week through the laboratory. . . . After all the data are collected, we call in the parents a class at a time and treat them en masse, referring the children to various clinics and explaining the importance of building latrines.

A Long Way from Solution

Our problem is still a long way from solution. Until the community starts its own latrine-building program, deparasitizing is of questionable value. (But as our lab technician said, "Every child deserves to be dewormed once in his life.")

Last spring we were given permission to vaccinate and immunize. Winny Evans . . . [another] public-health nurse, organized a crash program so that we could do the children before school was out. In the two months left in the school year, 600 *lycée* students received diphtheria-tetanus-typhoid immunizations, in a series of five shots, and 2,500 primary school children received diphtheria-tetanus immunizations, in a series of two shots. We were pleased with our results, and Winny then organized a summer program to immunize the preschoolers in the town, one *quartier* at a time. The chief of each *quartier* arranged matters so that on the appointed day his drummer was sent out tam-tamming the news around the streets. Mothers from other sections heard and came, too.

We stationed ourselves at a school, and so many women and children turned out that we called in the police to keep order. They came, took one look, and fled. We tried closing the doors, but babies were dropped in through the open window. At one point, I looked up and saw Winny Evans helplessly waving her syringe in the air, being carried off by a group of women. After her rescue, we then locked the doors, nervously smoked cigarettes, and listened to the acre of screaming women. Winny, always deadly calm when everyone else gets hysterical, announced that the "aims" of the program would have to be reviewed before we continued. I decided to review the "aims" of our mountain-climbing course, so that I could plot my exit over the roof. But fortunately our luck was with us that day, and a torrential rain clattered down upon the women, scattering them into empty classrooms. One brave policeman returned and blocked a door-way, then let the mothers out one by one. Thus we managed to finish the afternoon.

The following day we hired seven students to work with us, shout health-education tips to the mothers, keep them in line, and record the names of the children.

That program continued throughout the summer, but the star project of the season was the Dako demographic study started by Jean Hewitt.

No village in Togo had ever been studied thoroughly for its birth and death rates, frequency of diseases, family history, customs, and so forth. We chose Dako for its isolated site—we thought we'd have the inhabitants cornered—and because it was barnacled on a mountain overlooking a vast, spinach-colored valley, with sparkling rivulets running down the hills; and because its chief, Ouro Yerima, was wise and friendly and had an ostrich egg on the top of his hut to denote his importance.

We hired four Togolese *lycée* students to serve as interpreters and to work with the four Peace Corps teachers who came to do the interviewing. Our questionnaire was seven pages long.

On the chosen day, we loaded two Jeeps full of cots and *ignames* (a root crop which when boiled and dipped in hot sauce is called *fufu*), dignitaries, and brooms, and started the journey out on a road that also seemed to serve as a river bed during the rainy season. (It *was* the rainy season.) We were gravely received by the chief and the elders, who were seated under a great tree next to stone monuments erected in remembrance of ancestors. In the middle of the speechmaking, a part of the wall of the chief's compound collapsed. Everyone roared with laughter, and Nick hastened to hope that it was a good omen. It was.

We were housed in the school and presented with a goat, whom we named C. Payne Lucas, in honor of the acting Peace Corps representative. The goat's diet was one cigarette a day. Our diet was corn beef, antelope (which the hunters insisted was zebra), bam (a bamboo wine drunk out of thin, yellow calabashes), countless *ignames* and *gari* (another tuberous root, dried and ground to powder, then eaten with a sauce), which we cooked over a wood fire on an earthen floor, in a hut which we shared with chickens we got as gifts.

A Beautiful Summer

It was a beautiful summer. We interviewed every *concession*, a series of huts belonging to one chief, with his wives and children. Each is encircled by a wall, and all the buildings are a rich, soft red with thatched roofs and an occasional calabash vine crawling over them to give them the look of Easter hats.

On Thursdays the lab technicians and a doctor struggled out on the road and did physical exams and collected specimens. We did studies on all the inhabitants: blood, thick smear for malaria, stool-and-urine, and, for a selected group, anemia. The village was immunized, and World Health Organization workers did a leprosy-and-yaws study and vaccinated with smallpox.

The United Nations Food and Agricultural Organization sent out two nutritionists, Apolinaire and Agboton, to spend ten days in each of twenty households, weighing food before and after cooking and keeping track of the nutritional intake of each member of the family. At sunset they could be seen chasing through the millet fields some child who had decided to take his repast elsewhere, or sitting huddled in despair because the men of a certain household had gone to live in the fields, to protect their *ignames* from the gorillas.

At the end of the program of four months we were given one final dance, and on the morning of our departure the chief presented Jean and me with a tract of land where the villagers are now building us a *concession* so that we will come and live with them. Our best gift, however, we got upon returning a month later, when we found the head of each family had built a latrine as Nick had suggested. The results of the Dako project are to be published by WHO.

Life is very busy, quiet, and full. I moved some time ago to a little house *à l'indigène* with a thatched porch built by the Boy Scouts (in exchange for a guinea-hen dinner and guitar music) and four students—one Kabre, one Kotokoli, and two Moba— whom I house and feed. In exchange, they chase bats, fill lanterns, draw water, and pick mango pits out of the one flower bed. . . .

There are a few things which are terrible: one is night guard-duty at the hospital, which means you are usually up for twenty-four hours. This happens every sixth night or so. You cover the whole hospital, except maternity and surgery, alone. As you walk from building to building, your lantern strikes obstacles such as frogs and an occasional snake. There is no electricity after eleven o'clock, and putting in a chest tube or doing a spinal tap by flashlight is an experience to remember. . . .

The opportunity for creative nursing is endless. When we have Togolese counterparts to work along with us and see what it is we are trying to do with preventive medicine, our programs may continue after we leave.

My complaints seem as nothing, however, as I consider the poignancy of having a little one come up in the morning, curtsy, salute, and say *"bonsoir, monsieur."* It makes the banged-up knees, the school program, the never-ending line of . . . backs to shoot . . . an alive and important experience. Our job is almost baffling in its simplicity. It has been profoundly gratifying.

ENLARGING THE PEACE CORPS [6]

I am pleased to transmit legislation which will authorize the appropriation of $108 million for the Peace Corps in fiscal year 1964. [The Administration later reduced the request to $102 mil-

[6] From letter by the late President John F. Kennedy to Lyndon B. Johnson, then Vice President and president of the Senate, and John W. McCormack, speaker of the House of Representatives, July 4, 1963. *United States Department of State Bulletin.* 49: 170-2. Jl. 29, '63.

lion (see statement by R. Sargent Shriver, Jr., in the following article), and Congress appropriated $96 million in December 1963, a sum enabling the corps to enlarge its force to 10,500.— Ed.] . . .

In less than two years . . . [the Peace Corpsmen's] accomplishments have already been impressive. They constitute more than one third of all the qualified secondary teachers in Sierra Leone, Ethiopia, and Nyasaland; they have saved a three-quarter-million-dollar rice crop in Pakistan; they have vaccinated over 25,000 Bolivians; they are teaching in 400 Philippine schools; they have created a thriving poultry industry in the state of Punjab in India; they are teaching in every rural secondary school in Costa Rica and virtually every secondary school in British Honduras; they have contributed to the creation of a system of farm-to-market roads in Tanganyika. But these are only isolated examples; all over the world volunteers have surveyed roads, taught students and teachers, built schools, planted forests, drilled wells, and started local industries. In their off-hours they have conducted adult education classes, organized athletic teams, and launched programs ranging from music clubs to debating teams.

As important as these achievements are, they are far less important than the contribution Peace Corps volunteers are making in building those human relations which must exist for a happy and peaceful understanding between people. The United States and a few other fortunate nations are part of an island of prosperity in a world-wide sea of poverty. Our affluence has at times severed us from the great poverty-stricken majority of the world's people. It is essential that we demonstrate that we continue to be aware of the responsibility we fortunate few have to assist the efforts of others at development and progress.

With Americans, Lord Tweedsmuir [Scottish author and statesman who wrote under the name John Buchan] wrote, "the sense of common humanity is a warm and constant instinct and not a doctrine of the schools or a slogan of the hustings." By the careful selection and training of men and women in whom that instinct is a reality, the Peace Corps has already erased some stereotyped images of America and brought hundreds of thousands of people into contact with the first Americans they have ever known personally. "When the Peace Corps came to my country," wrote the minister of development of Jamaica, "they brought a breath of fresh air. They came and mixed with the people. They closed the gap and crashed the barrier. And because they did this, they have paved the way for our own people to understand. . . ."

It is no accident that Peace Corps volunteers have won this kind of acceptance. Nor is it a coincidence that they have been greeted—as the Ethiopian *Herald* stated—"with open arms." They have been warmly received because they represent the best traditions of a free and democratic society—the kind of society which the people of Africa, Asia, and Latin America long for as the ultimate end of their own revolution.

The Communist system can never offer men optimum freedom as human beings. The people of the world's emerging nations know this. Their aspirations for a free society are being stimulated by the presence of Peace Corps volunteers who have come not to usurp but to encourage the responsibility of local people and not to repress but to respect the individual characteristics and traditions of the local culture. "What is most remarkable about America," wrote [a] German scholar, Philip Schaff, "is that over its confused diversity there broods a higher unity." Because volunteers of different races and different religions nonetheless come from the same country, they represent the hope of building a community of free nations wherein each one, conscious of its rights and duties, will have regard for the welfare of all. . . .

The first American volunteers are already returning to the United States after two years of Peace Corps service. They are bringing home important skills and experience which will greatly enhance our knowledge of the world and strengthen our role in international affairs. More than one third of the seven hundred volunteers returning this year have indicated a desire to work in international programs. Their ability and usefulness is attested to by the action of thirty-five universities in the United States which have established two hundred scholarships for returning volunteers. One of these scholarships was created by the donations of the foreign students studying in California. I am also recommending a provision which would authorize the Peace Corps to assist these returning volunteers to make the most of their opportunities for further usefulness to the nation. [Such a provision was included in the 1963 amendments to the Peace Corps act.—Ed.]

PEACE CORPS SUCCESSES [7]

Two years ago Congress set forth three precise and clear goals for the Peace Corps:

1. To provide, to countries needing them, qualified volunteers who would help the people of these nations meet their needs for trained manpower;

2. To help provide a better understanding of the American people on the part of the people served;

3. To help provide a better understanding of other peoples on the part of all Americans.

On this third occasion of my appearances before your committee, Mr. Chairman, the Peace Corps has completed its first full cycle in pursuit of these objectives. On August 30, 1961, the first volunteers went overseas. They were a group of 50 teachers who have now completed their work in the secondary schools of Ghana and returned home. By January 1, approximately 700 volunteers will have completed two years of successful work. During 1964, another 3,000 will finish Peace Corps service.

These returning volunteers are the best evidence that the Peace Corps has grown from hope to reality. They are returning to tell of deep personal rewards, broadened understanding of world affairs, new friendships, and promising signs of achievement in education, agriculture, and community development in the countries where they have been serving. While many volunteers have found the work of helping nations to develop un-

[7] From Statement of R. Sargent Shriver, Jr., director of the Peace Corps. In *To Amend the Peace Corps Act;* hearings, October 15-16, 1963, on H.R. 8754. United States. Congress. House of Representatives. Committee on Foreign Affairs. 88th Congress, 1st session. The Committee. Washington, D.C. 20025. '63. p 3-8.

romantic and unglamorous, few, if any, have found it unimportant. They are making real accomplishments abroad.

Africa

Examples are found around the world. In Africa, volunteers have enabled many countries to increase vastly their school enrollments, to improve unmanageable pupil-teacher ratios, and to broaden and deepen curriculums. The importance of the presence of Peace Corps volunteers is apparent in such countries as Liberia, where volunteers account for 90 per cent of the degree-holding teachers, and Ethiopia, where they constitute well over one third of all secondary school instructors.

Latin America

Rural and urban community action programs involving Peace Corps volunteers in Latin America have achieved dramatic results in the area of public works. The material evidence of Peace Corps efforts is shown in the long list of projects initiated and completed with volunteer assistance.

In Colombia alone, this list includes the building of more than 100 schools and school kitchens, 30 aqueducts, 49 roads, and 14 bridges. Of course, none of this could have been achieved without the enthusiastic response of the Colombian people backed by their government, which has tripled its financial commitment to community action.

In Chile, 200 institutes called *centrales* instructing Chileans in all aspects of rural education have at least one volunteer each as a staff member. Of equal significance has been the formation in many Latin American countries of hundreds of 4-H Clubs whose young people are the key to their nation's future. There are lots of statistics on that.

Near East and South Asia

Many people were skeptical about what a handful of volunteers could do in a country as vast as India, with its population of over 450 million. But their impact has already been felt at the highest levels. As the first group recently prepared to come home from that nation, Prime Minister Nehru invited them to visit him. Word had reached him of the volunteers' success in a number of specific projects.

One volunteer had saved 40,000 citrus trees by demonstrating that radical pruning will bring them back to full production. More than 130 poultry units are now operating only because volunteers started them in the state of Punjab. Two volunteers established a machine shop which now makes farm implements in an area that imported them costly distances before; the volunteers are training Indians to make and sell these tools, and current orders are greater than can be filled in three months.

One small village has learned that its own effort, properly directed and used, could prevent the erosion of its fields and destruction of its houses for the first time in five seasons of monsoon assaults. A few volunteers have caused a quiet revolution in the utilization of books at a university. Previously the university sometimes had books locked up and the students were not allowed to use them.

These are the measurable accomplishments. But they represent efforts to fulfill only the first purpose of the Peace Corps Act and only a small part of our energies. The greatest achievements of the volunteers are in the area of personal relations.

Far East

The most outstanding single recognition of this so far is the presentation of the Ramón Magsaysay Award of $10,000 to the volunteers serving in eleven Asian nations. It was the first time the award—which is sometimes called Asia's equivalent of the Nobel Prize—has been conferred on a non-Asian group.

Its importance was pointed out in an editorial in the Manila *Evening News,* which said:

In twenty-two months of quiet labor, Peace Corps volunteers who came to this part of the world have secured a verdict not before vouchsafed to any other foreign group. Peace Corps workers achieved in less than two years an understanding with Asian peoples that promises to pass all tests.

I might just interpolate if I may here, Mr. Chairman, that I was in Manila to receive that award on behalf of the volunteers and I was talking to the members of the board of trustees of the foundation which gave the award. All of these trustees are Asians and they pointed out to me that nominations for the award are received from all sixteen countries which are defined by them to include Asia. When the nominations come in, the board of trustees screen them down to a manageable number, five or six. Then they go out and evaluate each of the potential recipients, because they want to be sure that the awards go to organizations or persons about whom there can be no question after the award is announced.

In the case of the Peace Corps, since we were working in eleven different Asian countries, the trustees of this foundation investigated the Peace Corps on their own initiative in all eleven countries. . . .

Latin America

Halfway across the world in South America a similar testimony was given last month to another group of volunteers. This recognition came in the form of "The Silver Medal of Arequipa" which was presented by Peruvian President Fernando Belaunde Terry to the forty-three volunteers working in Peru's second largest city. The award is given each year to the individual or group which has most helped the city of Arequipa—in this case, the volunteers, who were the first group of *norteamericanos* ever to receive the award.

If I may interpolate again, Mr. Chairman, there is another city in Peru called Cuzco, which used to be the ancient capital of Peru. They have a similar award in that city—I can't remember the exact title of it—but it is a medal, and that medal was given to the people working in Cuzco, in the mountains.

The examples I have cited illustrate why the measure of the Peace Corps achievement lies not in the fact that the number of volunteers has doubled each year, but in the understanding of a different way of life imparted by those volunteers and gained by them, and in the introduction of basic democratic principles of self-help and community organization in thousands of places throughout the world.

Number of Volunteers

As we have grown during the past year, Mr. Chairman, we tried to remember the admonition of your committee one year ago, that we "not try to go so fast that you will sacrifice efficiency.". . . Nor did we bring into service as many as we could have. Instead of reaching our estimate of 9,000 volunteers by August 31, we had on board on that date 6,634. . . .

Now, two reasons account for the difference. One is simply that we have deliberately applied higher standards to the selection of volunteers as the result of research and field experience showing what kind of person makes a successful volunteer. For example, greater stress is being placed upon language aptitude tests as a general predictor of success overseas.

We have doubled the amount of language training and raised standards of language competence. . . .

The second factor in the difference between our estimates and our present number of volunteers is the shortage of available people with certain skills in high demand overseas. We had requests for more than twice as many math and science teachers as we have sent abroad. The supply of trained agriculturalists also failed to meet what appears to be an insatiable demand. Other scarce skills are in great demand: engineers, geologists, doctors, and nurses, to name only a few.

The Peace Corps could have chosen to respond to requests for programs with skills which are more easily filled than those which the countries particularly requested. Or we could have chosen to relax our selection standards. Either choice would have enabled us to meet on time the estimates we made to you last year. In other words, it would have been very simple for us to have had 9,000 people on board August 31. But neither choice

Sargent Shriver, Jr., the Peace Corps director, to head it. Thus, would have produced the kind of Peace Corps you have enthusiastically supported the past two years.

We chose not to compromise. As a result, we had in service on August 31 some 2,300 volunteers less than we had planned, and we turned back to the Treasury some $3.9 million of unobligated funds as of June 30. . . .

I would like to mention that we could have obligated that money with the greatest of ease. It would have been a simple thing to spend every nickel that Congress appropriated to us, but we did not do so far the reasons I have just detailed.

This, of course, has caused us to review our estimates for the present fiscal year. The legislation before you seeks authorization for $108 million which would enable the Peace Corps to reach a level of 13,000 volunteers by next August. [See preceding article, letter by President Kennedy recommending this legislation.] While these goals—which were projected almost one year ago—are still possible, I do not believe they are realistic.

Our present proposal, therefore, is to have on board approximately 11,300 volunteers by next August, rather than 13,000. Having doubled in size during the past year while tightening standards of selection, I believe we can do almost the same this year. . . .

Reaching this goal of 11,300 volunteers will cost $102 million in fiscal year 1964 rather than the $108 million we proposed last fall when the President's budget was prepared and we had had only one year of actual experience in the field. You can be certain that if we do not reach this projected volunteer level, the unneeded funds will again return to the Treasury. [In December 1963 Congress appropriated a sum of $96 million for the Peace Corps, permitting it to expand to 10,500.—Ed.]

IV. EXTENDING THE PEACE CORPS IDEA

EDITOR'S INTRODUCTION

The impetus generated by the Peace Corps is illustrated by the many efforts at home and abroad to create other organizations modeled on it. Its vitality and success have stimulated various nations to organize their own units and have encouraged Americans to attempt to apply its principles in different ways. In October 1962 the United States Peace Corps sponsored the International Conference on Middle Level Manpower in San Juan, Puerto Rico, which reviewed the experiences of the corps. At the conference, attended by representatives of forty-three nations, delegates reported on their countries' policies and plans regarding national peace corps. By early 1964 eleven economically advanced nations had created units for overseas service and five less developed nations had set up their own domestic peace corps. As a result of the conference an International Peace Corps Secretariat with headquarters in Washington, D.C. was established to act as a clearinghouse for all peace corps.

In the United States, when Peace Corpsmen went into the slums of New York, homes of despondent older citizens, and rural communities of Puerto Rico to train under actual conditions for service abroad, the need for a domestic peace corps became obvious. Legislation providing for a National Service Corps to organize trained citizens for work in blighted and depressed areas and for a Youth Conservation Corps to use unemployed youth to improve the nation's forest and recreational areas was approved by the Senate in 1963, but was not voted on in the House of Representatives in that year.

The influence of the Peace Corps was also demonstrated by President Johnson's decision in 1964 to establish an agency, with a domestic peace corps and a job-training corps, to wage war on poverty in the United States and by his appointment of R.

the Peace Corps idea has been extended not only to disadvantaged nations, but also to disadvantaged people in prosperous nations: retraining, re-employing, rehabilitating those living in poverty amidst plenty.

The number of other suggestions for applying the Peace Corps idea has been growing because of the world-wide need to develop human skills and improve living conditions. Some of these proposals are considered in the following group of selections. They cover schemes for a National Service Corps, a Youth Conservation Corps, a United Nations peace corps, and a businessmen's peace corps.

DOMESTIC YOUTH SERVICES [1]

The future promise of any nation can be directly measured by the prospects of its youth. This nation—facing increasingly complex economic, social, and international challenges—is increasingly dependent on the opportunities, capabilities, and vitality of those who are soon to bear its chief responsibilities. Such attributes as energy, a readiness to question, imagination, and creativity are all attributes of youth that are also essential to our total national character. To the extent that the nation is called upon to promote and protect the interests of our younger citizens, it is an investment certain to bring a high return, not only in basic human values but in social and economic terms. . . .

Youth Employment

The employment prospects of youth depend on the general level of economic activity in the nation, as well as on specific efforts to increase opportunities for young persons. The high level of unemployment which the nation has experienced for the past five years has had sharply aggravated effects in this age group. . . .

[1] From *Our Nation's Youth;* message delivered by the late President John F. Kennedy to the House of Representatives on February 14, 1963. United States. Congress. House of Representatives. (H. Doc. no 66) 88th Congress, 1st session. Supt. of Docs. Washington, D.C. 20025. '63. p 2116-19.

My Committee on Youth Employment, consisting of Cabinet officers and distinguished public members, having studied these efforts and problems, has reported to me that the immediate need for additional youth employment opportunities is critical. The Administration's youth employment bill, which received wide endorsement when introduced in the Congress, is designed to meet this need.

Early enactment of this measure would spur Federal leadership and support to programs which would provide useful jobs and training for young persons who need them. The 1964 budget recommendations include $100 million in authorizations for the first year of this program, consisting of two distinct activities. First, a Youth Conservation Corps would be established, putting young men to work improving our forests and recreation areas. This would initially provide useful training and work for 15,000 youth. Second, the Federal Government will provide half the wages and related costs for young persons employed on local projects that offer useful work experience in nonprofit community services—such as hospitals, schools, parks and settlement houses. Forty thousand youths can be employed in the first year in this part of the program.

This bill is a measure of the first priority. The effects of unemployment are nowhere more depressing and disheartening than among the young. Common sense and justice compel establishment of this program, which will give many thousands of currently unemployed young persons a chance to find employment, to be paid for their services, and to acquire skills and work experience that will give them a solid start in their working lives.

I urge the Congress to enact at the earliest opportunity the Youth Employment Act which is so vital to the welfare of our young people and our nation.

National Service Corps

The youth employment bill should not be confused with a second important proposal—the National Service Corps. The youth employment program is designed for those young people who are in need of help—the unemployed, the unskilled, the unwanted. It is intended to boost the economy, to reduce unemployment, to train more young workers who would otherwise be idle. The National Service Corps, on the other hand, is designed for those citizens of every age, young and old, who wish to be of help—whose present skills, jobs or aptitudes enable them to serve their community in meeting its most critical needs, and whose idealism and situation in life enable them to undertake such an assignment on a volunteer basis. While it is conceivable that the type of projects assisted under these two programs could at times coincide, it is clear that their emphasis is wholly distinct. The youth employment bill will advance this nation's material wealth and strengthen its economy. The National Service Corps, which will not be limited to young people, will add to and make use of this nation's wealth of idealism and strengthen its spirit.

The logic and value of a National Service Corps has been demonstrated by the work and success of our Peace Corps overseas. . . . While admiring the work of these volunteers in carrying their skills and ideals to assist the needy in other lands, it is equally clear that the opportunities for service are also large here at home. Although the United States is the wealthiest nation the world has ever known, the poverty of millions of our people, and the need for training, assistance, and encouragement in numerous corners of our country, from teeming slum areas to those depressed rural areas virtually bypassed by technological and economic progress, provide fertile fields for those citizens with the desire and the ability to be of assistance.

Last November, I appointed a special committee to investigate the feasibility of applying the Peace Corps principle to the domestic scene. The committee consulted state, county and local officials and hundreds of organizations around the country, as well as the professional fields that would be most concerned with the use of volunteer workers. Its report, submitted last month, observing the cruel paradox that, within the richest and most powerful nation in the world, one sixth of our population lives on a submarginal level, recommended the creation of a voluntary service corps to help meet the problems of our own communities and citizens in distress. This is not only a constructive channel for youthful energy and idealism. Many of our senior citizens indicated their willingness to participate in this endeavor. The thousands of mature and able persons who stand ready to volunteer their services to improve community activities should be afforded the opportunity to do so.

Through the years millions of Americans have served their communities through the willing donation of their time and skill to voluntary private service organizations. But in a population growing in numbers, urbanization and the recognition of social problems, we need not only more professional personnel—more doctors, nurses, teachers and social workers—but an even greater number of dedicated volunteers to support the professional in every area of service.

I, therefore, recommend legislation to establish a National Service Corps—a small carefully selected volunteer corps of men and women of all ages working under local direction with professional personnel and part-time local volunteers to help provide urgently needed services in mental health centers and hospitals, on Indian reservations, to the families of migrant workers, and in the educational and social institutions of hard-hit slum or rural poverty areas.

This small task force of men and women will work in locally planned and initiated projects, at the invitation of community institutions, and under local supervision. The community's chief goal should properly be the development of the project to the point where local volunteers or paid staff workers could take over permanently the tasks initially undertaken by the corpsmen; and it is hoped that the example of men and women rendering this kind of full-time voluntary service would motivate many more Americans to participate on a part-time basis. This is not, I repeat, a constructive channel for youthful energy and idealism only. Many of our senior citizens indicated their willingness to participate in this endeavor.

A PEACE CORPS FOR OUR OWN BLEAK AREAS [2]

When President Kennedy, in 1960, outlined the idea of a Peace Corps that could be "building good will, building the peace," he seemed to reach directly into the hearts and minds of men and women throughout the country. He was articulating a feeling that had been spreading for some time—that this generation of Americans had a responsibility for the welfare of people of other nations, that many Americans wanted to do something positive and affirmative for peace. . . . In underdeveloped areas, the corpsmen have been bringing their skills and dedication to illiterate and impoverished people. More, they have been building self-reliance and friendships—the cornerstones of the free world.

It is this inspiring example of the overseas corpsmen that has had the President pondering whether Peace Corps concepts can be applied to our own bleak areas. Many senators, educators and civic leaders have been demanding a parallel organization—a domestic peace corps—for the impoverished at home. . . .

A preliminary report by a staff committee working in the past year under the attorney general states that there are "32 million persons . . . living at a lower level than America is capable of providing for its citizens." . . . There are many people just out of teacher-training institutes and the vocational schools, many highly skilled "retired" senior citizens, many with community development and farming skills, who might be helping other less fortunate Americans. There are also some 3 million people unemployed, including young men who feel rootless and frustrated by lack of opportunity. . . .

Is There a Need?

Many private studies have abundant evidence of a definite need at home—particularly among the so-called disadvantaged

[2] From article by Gertrude Samuels, New York *Times* correspondent. New York *Times Magazine*. p 34+. N. 25, '62. © 1962 by The New York Times Company. Reprinted by permission. (The article was written a year prior to the death of President Kennedy.—Ed.)

families and individuals in city and rural slums. There is very distinct worry over what James Bryant Conant calls the "social dynamite" that is building up in large cities in the form of jobless young people, "especially in the Negro slums." At the same time, there is a critical lack of personnel in both public and private agencies to undertake the wide variety of social and educational programs to change conditions and attitudes.

The needs are eloquently documented in recent reports by two important private groups: "Income and Welfare in the United States," by the Survey Research Center Institute for Social Research of the University of Michigan, which concludes that America is at the point "where poverty could be abolished"; and "Poverty and Deprivation in the U.S.," by the Conference on Economic Progress (comprising businessmen, economists, labor and farm leaders) which shows that two fifths of the nation is living under substandard conditions.

For example, living in poverty are almost 10.5 million families with annual incomes under $4,000, and almost 4 million people living alone who earn under $2,000—some 38 million Americans in all. Additionally, two thirds of all hired farm workers earn less than $1,000 a year. Living in "deprivation"—that is, short of minimum requirements for a modest standard of living—are another 10.3 million families. And chronic unemployment in urban and rural slums tends to freeze these millions at the bottom of the social ladder.

These experts believe that we cannot meet the challenge of the totalitarians by saying that the lowest tenth of our population lives better than nine tenths of the people of India. For new technology "makes persistent poverty intolerable by making it avoidable." The clear need is to raise substandard incomes through public policy—and to encourage, through public policy, a rehabilitation of the disabled and dependent.

The time is overdue, say many such experts, for far more extensive efforts in promoting more employment, improved education and health services, the development of natural resources and a great variety of other welfare programs. No private group can undertake all this. The best road, they say, lies through a centralized Federal service organization—a domestic peace corps —which could mobilize people with special skills, vigor and enthusiasm to (a) assist public agencies in expanding services at the community level and (b) augment the work of private agencies.

Senator Henry M. Jackson [Democrat] of Washington, who has supported the federally financed area-development program for depressed communities, put it bluntly the other day:

> So much of our society is affluent and we are having the highest standard of living in history—yet we have this terrible paradox of poverty for one segment of our people. This should aggravate all of us into doing more than we're doing. We're not just dealing with bricks and mortar.

How Would a Domestic Peace Corps Work?

Many great voluntary agencies have already pointed the way. They have a long tradition of performing valuable social and welfare services in depressed areas. But, as the attorney general's preliminary report states, they are limited. For example, the total number of social-work graduates last year for the whole country was 2,310, an all-time high. The noted New York School of Social Work dryly observes that this hardly makes a dent in the problem.

Sargent Shriver, director of the Peace Corps, adds: "No professional group will have enough social-work graduates in the next ten years." And social workers are only one of the many categories of skilled workers needed to lift up the deprived areas.

If the President decides to establish a domestic peace corps, there would probably be an initial phase for the sort of field training and orientation in social psychology that the overseas corpsmen have undergone. And just as with the overseas corpsmen, the domestic volunteers would not go to communities unless the local authorities asked for them.

It is also expected that they would serve on the same basis as those overseas—that is, on modest allowances for living costs plus a termination lump-sum payment. The selected areas would probably include the following:

On the urban scene: Corpsmen with teaching or vocational training experience would be valuable aides to education and employment. Many might work with school dropouts or embittered older people who neither have work nor know how to get it. As in Nigeria, where corpsmen have taken on semieducated groups and are stepping up the level of their interests, so . . . in [New York City]—in such areas as Bedford-Stuyvesant in Brooklyn or in East Harlem—they could provide tutoring, training and job counseling that would help youths and older people to look for work and hold their jobs.

Additionally, many more universities and colleges in the large cities may be expected to adopt the famous Antioch College concept of linking classroom education with field work in the slums. They could expand the Antioch approach to include vocational advisers, job-placement and recreation workers, home economists and caseworkers who would be expected to live and work on the job.

One such plan for New York City, for example, was detailed a year ago and sent to Washington by Ralph Whelan, then Commissioner of Youth Services and at present working with the Puerto Rican community. Fitting in well with the idea of a national Peace Corps, it proposed that volunteers from anywhere in the country should be recruited and screened for New York programs of delinquency prevention and treatment—a two-year work-and-study field program as part of their training for graduate degrees. Many experts see immense value in such an "exchange between states"—just as in international exchanges—to foster wider understanding.

On the rural scene: similar techniques could be applied with modifications. Migratory workers, for example, are among the most neglected in the country. The meager earnings of their young children (many of whom are victims of crippling accidents) are often needed for a family's survival. This luckless army of some 2 million people which harvests the crops that make

Americans the best-fed people in the world works on the rich California coast farms, in cotton and sugar-beet fields along the Mississippi and on East Coast farms from Florida to New Jersey and New York.

Peace Corps volunteers might work miracles with these forgotten Americans. They could help the migrants with good day-care programs. Nutritional aides could plan diets and dispense surplus commodities (as we have done in Peru). Teacher-aides could tutor the children who lag two to four years behind the national average. Mobile schools and libraries could accompany these families on the move. Experts could demonstrate the advantages of forming credit cooperatives so that the migrants would have access to reasonable-rate loans and not remain at the mercy of individuals who exploit them with high interest rates.

For another important rural group at the bottom of society—the American Indians—one fascinating pilot project has already been proposed to Washington by Dr. L. Mayland Parker, coordinator for Peace Corps training at Arizona State University.

Dr. Parker, an associate professor of agricultural economics, seeks a domestic Peace Corps which would help the impoverished Maricopa and Pima Indian colonies near Phoenix to improve their standard of living. He is asking for on-the-job instruction, accompanied by "such inspired enthusiasm" that it will encourage the Indians there—and eventually in other colonies—to develop self-reliance and community initiative. He wants the volunteers back-stopped with counterparts from the university faculty.

And to aid both urban and rural youth, many legislators have been fighting for a year to get a Youth Employment Opportunities Act passed. Blocked in the House, the bill will be brought up again at the coming session. They had sought to create a Youth Conservation Corps, along the lines of the old CCC camps, to provide healthful outdoor training and employment for thousands of young persons in the conservation and development of timber, soil and range. Additionally, it would have authorized public service training for some 25,000 urban young people.

It is not clear whether such a YCC would be made part of the national Peace Corps program. If not, corpsmen of all ages and skills might still have in it a leadership role—"as sort of platoon leaders of work cadres," says Senator Gale W. McGee [Democrat] of Wyoming, "where they would not only be helping communities, but also building the character of the youth."

Would the Corps Get Volunteers?

The reaction of many experts to this question and its variations—would it attract those with the right skills, right spirit, right thrust?—is that we can expect an overwhelmingly affirmative response . . . most experts interviewed agree with the attorney general's preliminary report that lack of trained people now working in the deprived areas coexists with the desire of many Americans who want "to serve but [have] no clear path to meaningful volunteer commitment."

Judge Justine Polier, nationally famous for her work with youth, is not one to mince words: "The most tragic waste is the destruction of the eagerness of our young people to serve the less fortunate."

Indeed, the response to the call is expected to be so overwhelming that, to many experts, it is not so much a question of whether a national corps would get recruits, but of how many should actually start the program. There are tens of thousands of young people—including those who responded to and could not be used in the limited overseas program—who can be expected to volunteer. There are thousands of socially conscious people, including the retired with independent wealth or special skills, who cannot for personal or professional reasons accept overseas posts but who would work for a moderate stipend at home. Their dedication and skills are going to waste.

Should it begin selectively, as did the overseas corps, with pilot projects of a few hundred or a thousand volunteers assisting in the city and rural slums? Or should it begin boldly, as Senator McGee envisages, aiming for 50,000 to 100,000 volunteers—and eventually absorb the thousands more young people who can be expected to join the YCC? Undoubtedly, questions like these will be thrashed out at the next session of Congress.

OPPOSITION TO A DOMESTIC CORPS [3]

A memorandum on the proposed Service Corps prepared by the staff of the Senate Republican Policy Committee devoted twice as much to "opponents' views" as it did to "proponents' views." The main argument cited against establishment of such a corps was that "a costly Federal program directed from Washington" offered a poor way to meet a need for local volunteers.

The concept that 5,000 Johnny Appleseeds skipping through the land and solving complex social problems with which 1,521,590 teachers, 133,051 professional social and walfare workers, 282,033 law enforcement officers and 200,999 members of the clergy have struggled for generations is . . . hardly a sound sociological solution.

The Senate Republican Policy Committee paper not only cited objections to the proposed Federal activity in areas of service traditionally within the province of state and local agencies. It also raised the question of whether volunteers working in an area where the national Government has pre-eminent responsibility—the Indian reservations—could add much to the services performed by the long-established Bureau of Indian Affairs in the Department of the Interior.

The Administration was criticized for linking the national service proposal to the Peace Corps, "thereby hoping to cash in on whatever enthusiasms may exist for the foreign Peace Corps." The problems and solutions in the two areas of service, the recital of "opponents' views" said, were not comparable. The typical underdeveloped country has limitless needs; it lacks basic institutions for service, and few of its people are able or willing to volunteer needed services. Its situation hardly compares with that of the United States, where there are any number of public and private welfare programs and an already large number (estimated at 22 million) of citizen volunteer workers. Opponents

[3] From "Domestic Peace Corps," by Helen B. Shaffer, staff writer, *Editorial Research Reports*. *Editorial Research Reports*. 1:253-5. Ap. 3, '63. Reprinted by permission.

of the plan were said to suspect that, as the original Peace Corps was aimed at making friends for the United States in newly independent countries, the domestic corps would be expected "to sell the New Frontier" to U.S. voters.

Criticism of the plan has not been limited to Republicans. Senator Frank J. Lausche . . . [Democrat of Ohio] attacked the "so-called domestic Peace Corps" on the floor of the Senate, Feb. 6 [1963]:

> We have legions of Peace Corps workers already in our country . . . the ministers, priests, and rabbis; the parents, . . . teachers, . . . social workers, . . . recreational workers, . . . the police and juvenile court officials. . . . We are reaching the point where we will have more guides working for government than we have people to guide.

Lausche's attack stemmed from his objections to a Federal grant of $250,000 to help finance a program to train volunteers for the fight against juvenile delinquency in New York City's Harlem section. The grant was one of two score made by the Department of Health, Education and Welfare under authority of the Juvenile Delinquency and Youth Offenses Control Act of 1961. The Harlem project has no connection with the national service program, although its local sponsors publicized it as "the first domestic Peace Corps." The Ohio senator objected specifically to the Harlem project's $157,000 payroll. His colleague, Senator Stephen M. Young . . . [Democrat of Ohio], joined in urging that "We should carefully scrutinize the proposal for a so-called domestic Peace Corps [National Service Corps] before we embark on still another program which will cost millions of taxpayers' dollars."

A UNITED NATIONS PEACE CORPS [4]

The essential concept of the Peace Corps is simple—simple to state, that is—and immensely difficult to administer effectively.

[4] Address, "Internationalizing the Concept of the Peace Corps," delivered by Harlan Cleveland, Assistant Secretary of State for International Organization Affairs, before the Washington Council of the Experiment in International Living, Washington, D.C., March 28, 1961. *United States Department of State Bulletin.* 44:551-2. Ap. 17, '61.

It involves recruiting skilled and dedicated people, mostly in their twenties; screening and training them rigorously, with emphasis on developing their cultural empathy, their sense of organization, and their perception of the America from which they come; and then putting them to work as additional help in existing organizations already engaged in the economic and social development process in the less developed areas—in U.S. aid missions, in American voluntary agencies, in the host governments themselves, and in international agencies.

But when you think through what it means to put young Americans in international agencies, some difficult and interesting questions crop up. Don't we have to assume that, if Americans are put into these agencies in considerable numbers, other countries will feel that they should do the same? Don't we have to assume that the Soviets, who have copied most of the other major initiatives in American foreign policy since World War II (including the Marshall Plan, the European integration drive, and the Point Four program), will copy this one too? Can we foresee the time when little bands of Komsomols [members of Russian Communist youth organization] will be coexisting competitively with the American Peace Corps?

If the probable answer to these questions is yes, why not plan from the outset on an international peace corps in addition to the American effort that is already under way?

The case for an international approach to technical assistance —that an international agency can participate more deeply and more relevantly in a sovereign government's economic and social planning, that internationally administered aid removes the sting of cross-cultural domination from the always ticklish relationship between donor and recipient—also makes a strong case for internationalizing the peace corps idea. Indeed, such an idea is already being tried out on a small scale: dozens of Dutch youngsters are serving internships in the Food and Agriculture Organization and other UN agencies all over the world. The more we can export our good will and good intentions through international agencies, the easier it will be for the new countries, particularly those very sensitive, very new countries in Africa, to import the technical help they need without its being regarded merely a form of imperialism—either the nineteenth century colonial or the twentieth century Kremlin variety.

If we start thinking in terms of an international peace corps as well as an American one, it is not difficult to project some of the needs for more junior help in the international technical assistance programs. Suppose we can develop some machinery under the [United Nations] Economic and Social Council to recruit and build international teams in which American youngsters would work alongside of British, French, Russians, Brazilians, Japanese, Indians, and others. Here, for example, are some of the ways these international peace corps volunteers might be used:

1. In the case of the United Nations' own operations they might serve as staff assistants and technicians' helpers in support of particular UN programs. At present the work of the UN resident representatives responsible for the Expanded Technical Assistance Program and Special Fund activities is severely handicapped by lack of office help of every kind, from "leg men" to typists, messengers, and chauffeurs. The volunteers could also help in the growing amount of work involved in developing statistical services and in the expanding business of community development in many lands.

2. The UNESCO [United Nations Educational, Scientific and Cultural Organization] education program, which is going to concentrate in Africa this next year or two, could use peace corps volunteers as teachers or teachers' helpers, could put some of them to work in the actual building of schools with native materials, using cheap and efficient designs that have already been worked up. For some volunteers a particularly exciting prospect might be to help in the archaeological digs in the upper Nile Valley, part of UNESCO's attempt to save some of the Nubian monuments that will otherwise be lost forever under the waters that pile up behind the Aswan Dam.

3. The International Labor Organization, so its director general has just told us, could make effective use of volunteers in its manpower training programs on the lower intermediate level and in its share in community development programs—for example, in the Andean-Indian program.

4. The World Health Organization could offer a chance to participate in its widespread malaria eradication and sanitation efforts and in the child health centers which it is developing together with the Children's Fund [UNICEF].

5. The Food and Agriculture Organization is already using volunteers from the Netherlands and could use a great many more in several of its operating programs, notably the fight against animal diseases, locust control, and some phases of agricultural extension work and food preservation.

The work will not be easy. It doesn't take very much skill, but it does take a good deal of dedication to go out into the countryside jabbing the flanks of animals with inoculation needles or spraying hovels with DDT. But for Americans to do these things in company with people from other countries would doubly intensify the experience and help a whole generation of Americans learn not merely how to work *for* but how to work *with* other people.

So if we think the peace corps idea is a good one—and by the hundreds of thousands we obviously do—let's experiment with it in our international institution building. As a change from the cold war, as a change from the dreary and unnecessary debates over Cuba's wild charges and the Kremlin's bitter attacks on the UN—as a change from all this cold-war maneuvering—let us experiment with a hot peace instead. Why wouldn't a proposal for a United Nations Peace Corps be a good place to start?

BUSINESSMEN ORGANIZED FOR PEACE [5]

I would like to put forth a personal proposal for action. It is my suggestion that private companies in the industrialized nations—in addition to pursuing their own investment opportunities abroad—volunteer to send members of their management to work in the developing areas.

[5] From address, "Managerial Work and Human Progress," delivered by David Rockefeller, president of the Chase Manhattan Bank, New York, September 16, 1963, before the Comité International de l'Organisation Scientifique 13th International Management Congress, organized by the Council for International Progress in Management (USA), Inc. Copyright © 1963 by the Comité International de l'Organisation Scientifique. Reprinted by permission.

I have in mind what might be called a Managerial Task Force of Free Enterprise. Its volunteers would serve for periods of perhaps two or three years in a unit assigned to a particular nation. They would be on leave of absence from their companies in Western Europe, North America, Japan or elsewhere, but would continue to receive full salary and fringe benefits from these companies. Under no circumstances would they be forced upon a nation against its will. They would go only by invitation, and would work on the planning and organizing of special projects deemed essential to national economic development.

Suppose, for example, that a country's development plans called for building a major textile mill. One unit of volunteers might be assigned to get this project under way and oversee its operation through the difficult formative period. Or an established company might be encountering problems of production, marketing or cost control on which a unit could contribute helpful recommendations. Or such a unit might be given the job of aiding local schools in setting up business courses, of organizing advanced management institutes, or of inaugurating in-service manager training programs to help talented nationals advance to positions of increasing responsibility.

The initiative for such a volunteer program, it seems to me, could quite properly come from a respected world-wide management organization of the stature of CIOS (Comité International de l'Organisation Scientifique). It has the facilities to organize units on a global basis, as well as the prestige to insure maximum cooperation from business, government and those agencies of the United Nations already active in the field of management training.

Private industry should welcome the opportunity to participate. For not only would these volunteers make an immediate social contribution, but they would also gain experience that would be invaluable to their companies and themselves in the future. In the selection of candidates, I would hope that a company would send not the man it could easily do without today, but the man it surely could not do without tomorrow.

Obviously, I have sketched this idea in broadest terms. Any such proposal inevitably would involve formidable problems of procedure, of equity, and of government and corporate policy. It would require the closest supervision, country by country, to make sure it was contributing effectively in breaking the shackles of backwardness. But I believe the basic concept has enough merit to justify further examination of its usefulness to our society.

V. EVALUATION

EDITOR'S INTRODUCTION

A final and complete evaluation of the Peace Corps would be a premature undertaking. Little more than three years old, this organization of some 7,000 men and women is charged by Congress with advancing "world peace and friendship." Its specific functions are to provide qualified Americans to help raise living standards in developing nations, to give Americans a better understanding of conditions in other parts of the world, and to promote among other peoples a better understanding of Americans and American democracy.

Considering the problems it faces, the United States Peace Corps appears all too small a body. President Kennedy had hoped that by the end of 1964 there would be 13,000 Peace Corpsmen to carry out its mission, but as of December 1963, Congress had provided funds for only 10,500. Although there are other United States Government agencies seeking to improve conditions in developing nations, the Peace Corps, granted the small scale of its operations, has been considered the most effective. Nonetheless, it is often necessary to placate the corps' opponents by relating it to narrow interests instead of a more universal purpose. Thus, whether or not the Peace Corps program can be enlarged to provide genuine remedies for some of the causes of war—poverty, disease, illiteracy, misunderstanding, outmoded technology—remains to be seen.

The material contained in the earlier sections of this book forms the basis of a preliminary general evaluation; the following selections, however, set forth several views on the specific weaknesses and strengths of the Peace Corps. The major shortcomings discussed are the corps' inability to attract volunteers with certain scientific skills and the difficulty of increasing its numbers. Its principal contributions, as pointed out below, are its ability to organize grass-roots democratic activities, the creation of a close emotional rapport with foreign peoples, the example it provides of foreign assistance carefully designed to meet the specific needs of each country, and its infusion of American youth once again with the spirit and values of the American Revolution and the frontier.

OBJECTIVE: LOCAL DEMOCRATIC ACTION [1]

A New Theory of Foreign Aid

The starting point of this theory, on the negative side, is the conviction that the West cannot counter the effect of Red agitators in underdeveloped nations either by shoring up central-government operations of these nations, or by investing massively in construction of dams, highways, seaports, airports, and the like. On the positive side, the theory rests on the claim that the best hope of the West lies in the possibility of transforming masses of rural folk—people long afflicted by a sense of total powerlessness —into men conscious of a capacity to alter their lives by local democratic action.

Proponents of this new theory do not deny that the tens of billions of American dollars funneled into capital investment abroad, through the ICA and other agencies, have strengthened the economies of the nations involved. They believe, however, that money spent in this way does more for the Communist contriver of chaos than for the friend of the West. For while some of its effects trickle down, a quantity of hard cash clings to central-government fat cats and fortune builders. And the latter are easy marks for agitators working among back-country villagers who lack all sense of local identity and live in swamps of bitterness or apathy.

That a small, back-country project is necessarily much better does not follow from this, of course. But, according to the new

[1] From "The Peace Corps' Secret Mission," by Benjamin DeMott, professor of English, Amherst College. *Harper's Magazine.* 223:63-8. S. '61. Reprinted by permission of the author.

theorists, something uniquely valuable can be made of such projects, provided the emphasis is not simply on physical improvements. If community effort on a drainage ditch or a schoolhouse develops structures of local power out of emptiness—if it issues in village governments functioning on representative lines—it may well have a value proportionally greater than that of a huge urban hospital or a major hydroelectric installation. For the completed schoolhouse is not then merely another square hard object added to the surface of the earth. It is a sign of change in psychological landscape—a living, growing obstacle in the path of agitators who flourish in a power vacuum.

Easy analogies between frontier life in the United States and village life in the emergent countries are not acceptable to the new theorists. They are certain, though, that Tocqueville and other early observers were right to see a connection between the stability of the American system and our national habit of voluntary association at the local level. And they are impatient with ironical, supersubtle views of small-town organizations in this country. Satirists chuckle as these organizations—clusters that include not only Boards of Selectmen, Town Meetings, School Committees, and PTA's, but dozens of "chapter" organizations: Boy Scouts, Lions, Rotary, Chamber of Commerce, Garden Club, League of Women Voters, and others. In contrast, the new theorists believe in dead earnest that these institutions, meeting regularly and electing officers year by year, are powerful influences upon the development of a community sense of the style and meaning of democracy.

What is more, they believe this style *is* communicable.

In their view, young Americans of intelligence and sensitivity can do more than dig ditches and operate tractors for the people of the underdeveloped countries. They can help these people to feel their way toward the reality of the democratic institution as a self-made order, with its own limits, tensions, and requirements in the way of patience and restraint. They can do all this, can function as guides for emergent local democracy, if the lessons to be taught are not taught in a void.

This means that instead of offering condescending lectures on "citizenship," they must find a vital local project that can serve as a laboratory. The kind of project best adapted to this purpose is currently described as one of "community development." The idea of community development has a long history filled with saints and politicos—Gandhi among them. For American intellectuals the idea is closely associated with the name of Paul Goodman, author of the recent *Growing Up Absurd* and other works of social criticism. Public servants, however, are more likely to cite Richard Poston as the American pioneer in refining the concept. An intense, wiry, witty research professor at Southern Illinois University (rarely in residence), Poston is an unpublicized consultant to foreign governments and private international agencies in the United States who has become a figure of some influence on aid and development policy within the last five years. A vigorous critic of ICA programs, Poston defines the aims of a community development project as, on the one hand, "evolving socially responsible individual traits," and, on the other, developing "all community functions and institutions that are essential to a strong democratic society." To the charge that the quotient of idealism in the theory is impossibly high, his scoffing retort is: "Look at the numbers."

Thousands of New Village Governments

The numbers Poston has in mind are, beyond doubt, enormously impressive. In India, for instance, a prime minister's committee began a community development program 9 years ago—a pilot project covering 27,388 villages, each with its village-level worker. In 4 years the project was extended to 10 times that many villages (with a population of 150 million), and it is scheduled to cover all rural areas in the country by the fall of 1963. The Philippines instituted a similar program 4 years ago; by now more than 1,500 trained village-level workers have led in the completion of numberless civic-improvement projects and helped to establish 23,000 local village governments. And there are comparable programs in Iran, Israel, Puerto Rico, Colombia, and elsewhere.

The pattern of action varies from country to country and from section to section within a country. In one village, local institutions or elective offices may have existed at some time in the past —before, say, the ravages of civil war. In another there may never have been any local self-definition whatever, only a blank filled by some distant appointive authority understood by villagers to be remote, mysterious, and corrupt. Normally the community development worker begins by encouraging the simplest forms of cooperative enterprise—toward any end that stirs the imagination of the villagers with whom he talks. He does not dictate out of his sense of "the real local needs." Neither does he seek outside help at the start. His first job is to bring villagers together as a group conscious of itself, and concerned to act positively toward a specific end. In undertaking this job, though, he has clearly in mind that his final purposes are to shape community attitudes, to encourage habits of democratic decision and representative action, and to develop understanding of the idea of elective authority. He reads his success not in a completed building but in evidences of a new community stance toward local issues and problems.

Petitions for Light

A Colombian barrio of sixty families, a primitive place called Guacimalito, was the scene of a recent achievement in this line. (The tale is one of many told at length in a privately published CARE report on community development in Colombia.) Local farmers marketed their produce in the country's second largest city, Medellín. Though the needs of their village were endless— clear water was one—the farmers, wide-eyed at the wonders of the city, saw no need as pressing as that of procuring electric light. A few of them had even gone so far as to hire a sort of floating lobbyist from another town to plead for them before the light commission.

At about the time of this venture, training teachers from a nearby school arrived to set up literacy classes. After the fashion of community development workers, they organized regular meetings of the townspeople and encouraged the latter to act for themselves in the matter of electricity, advising them to circulate a petition to be presented to the commission. The petition was circulated and presented—an action that marked the first time that local people had represented their own interest to officialdom.

Officialdom was not much interested in their interests, to be sure. The commission allowed that the barrio was low on the list, and that in any case it would be impossible to bring power trucks through to them—there was no road to the place from the highway. This turn of events produced more meetings, more petitions, and at length a concrete proposal, from the village leaders themselves, that the families of the town build the necessary access road and offer to dig the holes for the telephone poles—provided the authorities would show them where to dig. The proposals were approved and work was begun. A neighbors' committee was formed to look into other projects; a plan was approved calling for petitions about an aqueduct for clean water; memoranda were prepared to be sent to the governor of the province asking for auxiliary police; citizens were appointed to conduct a barrio survey and census, which they did.

It is one thing to organize, another to achieve: government response to the villagers' initiative came slowly in all instances. But it was forthcoming. And the machinery developed for local action has not broken down. Its future is uncertain, of course, but even if the worst happened, the political experience of these villagers would remain a shade more complicated than it might otherwise have been. In a place where most people were apathetic or fearful, a functioning, representative village "administration" has come to exist. The villagers have proved, in the face of the claims of agitators or terrorists, that they themselves are capable of effecting significant improvements in their immediate environment. And that proof will be difficult to expunge from local memory.

[It will be] especially difficult . . . in those villages where the conduct of several "single-action" projects has been directly connected with the emergence of a distinct political unit with its own style. In recent months Hojas Anchas, a mountain *vereda* (or roadside settlement) in the Andes *municipio* of Supia, Caldas, has completed a boy's school, a public-health post, a jail. It has also set up a local government with some rituals of its own. The Colombian survey reported six months ago that:

> Saturday night in Hojas Anchas the Vereda Junta meets from six to eight to discuss . . . ongoing projects, finances, future plans, etc. . . . Whether or not the priest is present the meeting goes on. After the elected president opens [it], there is a Scripture reading, then notes of the previous meeting are read and approved. Then the order of the day is read, and comments are asked from the floor. . . . Sixty-three adults make up the junta and [its] board of officers [is] elected each year. Requisites for belonging to the junta, strictly adhered to, are broken down into obligations and rights. . . .

The key obligation, set forth flatly, is: "Majority decisions must be respected by all." The key right is: "Anyone who has a problem must be listened to by the others."

Colombia's recent history lends special urgency to efforts like these. A twelve-year-old civil war has killed three hundred thousand; violence has centered in village-level conflicts. In 1957 a national plebiscite approved a constitutional reform calling for alternate four-year periods of rule by Conservatives and Liberals until 1974; an orderly transfer of power from president to president in that period plainly depends upon rapid growth in political maturity.

But the political situation in Colombia can hardly be described as unique among underdeveloped nations. The fact is that experience of civic action and responsibility is equally urgent in virtually all the countries that have shown interest in the Peace Corps. Whether sick or well, hungry or full, the people of these nations cannot judge the way of freedom unless they have an inkling of what that way is like—an inkling that no hospital or highway or sleek government Cadillac can possibly provide for them. And all available evidence indicates that much more can be done to provide them with this inkling than anyone originally suspected. . . .

E. Gordon Alderfer, assistant executive director of CARE, is strongly committed to the principles of community development, and has written about it as an effort toward "a maturation of responsible citizenship." While the [Peace Corps] volunteers were at Rutgers this summer, they were taught by Richard Poston himself, retained by CARE to explain to them how they can best do a job which, in Poston's words, is primarily that of stimulating people "to think and plan for themselves and to execute their own . . . decisions." Moreover, the corpsmen will be paired off in the field with Colombians who have been specially trained for the program of "Acción Comunal"—a national version of community development already launched in Colombia. The broad task of Acción Comunal workers is to lead their countrymen toward an intuition of the difference between victims and citizens. And the chance is good that they will not only accept but expect advice from young Americans who bring to local projects both technical expertise and the experience of people who from birth have been participants in democratic institutions.

Elsewhere, though, the prospect is far less bright—and not because Colombia is unique in needing something more than mere improvement in the quality of physical life. Tanganyika . . . has not been torn by a decade of civil war. But it is a new nation. . . . And it is beset by serious problems of bureaucratic and political organization. Desperately poor, it has had to allocate millions of dollars to hire civil servants from outside— for lack of Africans with even minimum experience in civil procedures. Committed (for the future) to the British political system, the country is now run by a prime minister whose "party" holds all but one seat in the national assembly; dissident forces are reportedly too inexperienced in politics to organize themselves as a functioning opposition. In light of all this, it is hard to believe that the Peace Corps' potentials for the development of local government and for joint civic action are less relevant in Tanganyika than elsewhere.

THE PEACE CORPS WINS ITS WAY [2]

In its early days, it seemed almost fashionable to pounce on the Peace Corps. There was a torrent of abuse from self-styled "realists," anti-foreign-aiders, Southern Democrats, conservative Republicans, and opponents of Government spending. Among those who spoke harshly of the new organization was former President Eisenhower. He scoffed at the corps as a "juvenile experiment" devised to spend money wastefully.

Yet many who started by carping have ended by praising. One of the best-known converts is Senator Barry Goldwater, the Republican Party's high priest of conservatism, who once predicted that the corps would be a haven for a "bunch of beatniks who wouldn't work." More recently he reversed his stand, concluding, "I think the Peace Corps is beginning to remove the doubts from the doubters' minds . . . I'll back it all the way."

Another impressive change in attitude is that of Representative Howard W. Smith, the conservative Virginia Democrat who heads the House Rules Committee. Smith voted against the corps originally but reported this year, "I have taken care to read what I could about the performance of this program as it went along, and I am happy to say that I think they have done a good job."

Senator Russell Long, Louisiana Democrat, was so incensed by an entertainer's satiric song poking fun at the Peace Corps that he stood up in a Washington night-spot and gave the surprised audience a lecture on the value of the organization.

Emphasizing the change in climate is the willingness of members of Congress to back up their words with votes. Last year [1961], in its first test on the Peace Corps, the House approved establishment of the agency 285 to 97. In April of this year, despite the fact that authorization for a budget of $63,750,-000, twice the first year's appropriation, was at stake, the vote was 316 to 70.

[2] From article by Thomas W. Ottenad, Washington correspondent, St. Louis *Post-Dispatch*. *Progressive*. 26:19-22. Ag. 62. Reprinted by permission.

While it is still early to measure tangible accomplishments, the promise of the first year and a half is encouraging. There are indications that the Peace Corps may produce beneficial effects on United States relations with underdeveloped nations. It may also point the way to new directions in foreign aid and foreign policy and provide a future pool of competent manpower for the State Department and other Government agencies.

The Peace Corps could well have a twofold impact on American relations with the countries of Latin America, Africa, and Asia. On the one hand, the presence of idealistic, hard-working young Americans should do much to give emerging nations a truer understanding of the United States and its people. On the other, the presence of Americans as schoolteachers and advisers and as helpers in agricultural and community development projects in these young countries should encourage the growth of democratic institutions.

It will be years before long-range effects of this kind may emerge. There have been minor developments already, however, which show that the corps is winning a place for itself abroad. Thus:

In Tanganyika recently, when the corps was attacked by a member of parliament, Premier R. M. Kawawa immediately came to its defense. He praised the work being done by a group of American engineers and geologists and reaffirmed his government's hope of obtaining more corpsmen.

A newspaper in Pakistan made this significant comment in welcoming a Peace Corps group to that country last October: "Mr. Dulles had his brinkmanship. Mr. Kennedy has his peacemanship."

A newspaper in the Philippines, observing that the United States frequently displays its worst side both at home and abroad, credited the Peace Corps with creating "a new American image," and added that "it is a heart-warming one."

Dr. Akhter Hameed Khan, director of the Academy for Village Development in Comilla, East Pakistan, [See "Librarian in the Peace Corps," section II, above.] praised eight corpsmen assigned to the institution for giving technical competence and youthful vigor in training mechanics and improving farming, irrigation methods, and community life. "They are doing something that would not have been done at all or would have been done only under exceptional circumstances and at very great cost," he said.

Last spring a Nigerian newspaper called on its government to abolish its army and establish a Nigerian Peace Corps instead.

None of these incidents in themselves is likely to have any appreciable effect on American relations with the nations involved. They illustrate, however, that the corps is creating a new kind of emotional rapport with foreign countries. In time, what is now essentially a limited, personal relationship could become the basis for a better kind of international friendship that the United States could not achieve by traditional diplomacy.

The Peace Corps may well turn out to be the right kind of operation in the right place at the right time. At the heart of the corps is a concept of limited assistance on simple but essential economic and social self-help projects. This approach may prove peculiarly valuable for countries whose economic and political systems are in an elementary stage unsuited to massive infusions of capital or sophisticated aid of the type that the Marshall Plan gave to the advanced countries of Western Europe. . . .

Requests received so far show an interesting pattern of need among underdeveloped areas. In Africa the great clamor is for teachers. In Latin America the call is for help in community improvement work, first in rural areas and small villages but with increasing emphasis on the slums of big cities. In the Near East and southern Asia, projects frequently tend to be multipurpose, merging agricultural extension work with health and education activities. In every case Peace Corps recruits are intended as a source of working manpower. They are not advisers. They are workers providing skills and knowledge that are in short supply. . . .

There are 26 corpsmen working on an agricultural program in India. A training class conducted by two volunteers to teach poultry raising is reaching two hundred trainees, who will in turn pass their knowledge on to others in 8 to 10 villages each. Seven volunteers are teaching informal classes in sheet metal work, welding, workshop methods, and English. Two are organizing youth groups with a total membership of six hundred boys.

Malaya has a complement of 67 Americans engaged in rural development, health, and education projects. Ten volunteers teach more than 1,000 Malayan students in biology, mathematics, general science, commercial subjects, and vocational trades. Nurses and medical technicians work in rural health centers, laboratories, and a leprosarium, and teach classes in public health.

Adding to the value of these undertakings is the fillip of individual achievement by some Peace Corps members whose ingenuity and enthusiasm have carried them far beyond their formal assignments. In Colombia a member of the corps invented a loom for weaving bamboo strips to be used in a simple method he devised for reinforcing structural concrete. In Pakistan a recruit invented a machine that parboils rice cheaply and efficiently so that it can be husked more easily. A volunteer in Thailand won wide popularity when he held a Thai boxer to a draw in an exhibition match fought Eastern-style, complete with kangaroo kicks and other unfamiliar tactics. . . .

Although only a neophyte, the Peace Corps has devised effective ways of averting the "ugly American" label so common among overseas personnel. Its chief weapons are tight purse-strings and strict orders to its members to adapt to local customs and mores. Instead of a salary, members of the corps receive allowances intended to enable them to live on the same plane as their local counterparts. Varying with the cost of living abroad, they range from a low of $63 a month in India to a high of $168 in Tanganyika. In two countries allowances were cut when it was found the initial figures were too high. . . .

The agency's officials, who have charge of missions in each country, are better paid. Annual salaries range from $6,035 to

$18,450, depending largely on the size of the project. Mission directors also receive allowances to cover the cost of housing and part of the expense of education for their children. They get none of the cost of living allowances, hardship salary differentials, and other fringe benefits that often make overseas living luxurious for other Government personnel. They are directed to stay off the cocktail circuit and out of American residential compounds.

Perhaps the major accomplishment of the Peace Corps so far is the unparalleled, enthusiastic acceptance it has won from foreign countries. Nearly every nation where missions are operating has asked for more corpsmen, with some nations seeking to quadruple their present forces.

The source of some of the requests is rather surprising. Nigeria . . . [has asked for] 400 more teachers to add to the 109 it now has. Ghana, whose President Kwame Nkrumah received the Lenin peace prize from the Soviet Union this spring, has requested 185 additional teachers to supplement 51 already sent there.

Despite its success, the corps' operations have revealed some shortcomings. One of the most important is its consistent failure to attract sufficient recruits with certain types of skills. It has been chronically short of mathematics and science teachers, engineers, agricultural specialists, nurses, social workers, and skilled craftsmen. As a result, some projects have been delayed or cut back.

There have been administrative bobbles, most of them relatively minor in nature. A certain amount of confusion still marks operations of the organization's headquarters. Slowness in completing preliminary medical examinations and character investigations has caused inconvenience for some volunteers who were allowed to begin training only to be dropped later when the checkup produced unsatisfactory results. Some corpsmen have complained that the training they received did not equip them adequately for their assignments.

But whether as the result of good fortune, good planning, or the ability and stamina of its predominantly young recruits, members of the corps seem to have adapted well to life in alien lands. Only three have had to be recalled for failure to fit satisfactorily into foreign assignments. Only one incident, the Nigerian postcard episode, has caused friction abroad, and even that was short-lived. [A volunteer criticized local standards of living on a postcard which was seen by Nigerian students. Their protests led to her recall.—Ed.] While many corpsmen have suffered dysentery and other illnesses, there has been only one death from disease. Two other volunteers lost their lives in a plane crash in Colombia.

What the future holds for the Peace Corps depends largely on how effectively it operates at the grass-roots level overseas for long months and years after the initial excitement and enthusiasm have faded. Much will depend, too, on whether the benefits it brings can be made to last after the corpsmen have gone home. Some of its undertakings, like community self-improvement programs, are based on concepts difficult for impoverished, uneducated peasants to understand. In some cases natives are said to be willing to work as long as Peace Corps members are on the job but show little desire to carry on by themselves.

Increasing harassment by Communists is almost certain to become a major problem in the future. As the corps grows larger and becomes more effective, the Communists, who already have branded it an arm of imperialism and a wing of the Central Intelligence Agency, are expected to attack it with greater vigor.

Much of the credit for the corps' initial success goes to its director, R. Sargent Shriver, a brother-in-law of President Kennedy, and his hardworking, capable staff. Shriver is a do-it-now activist who slashed Government red tape to bits in starting the corps. Warren W. Wiggins, thirty-nine-year-old associate director, is credited by Shriver with being largely responsible for the successful planning and organization of the agency.

While the Peace Corps is important as one of the few bold innovations of the Kennedy Administration, its implications for the future are both practical and dynamic. It indicates that programs of relatively modest size, if tailored to fit the social and economic needs of other countries, may in some cases be a more effective kind of foreign aid—helping people to help themselves—than lavish but ill-suited handouts of military or financial assistance. As one member of the corps suggested recently, in some underdeveloped countries a group of Peace Corps volunteers may be worth more than a shiny new steel plant or a dam.

UNSENTIMENTAL JOURNEY [3]

The Americans who converged on Monrovia [Liberia] in April [1963] for three days of meetings might easily have been mistaken for young corporate executives planning a new business campaign in Africa. In this instance the corporation was the American Peace Corps and the young executives its directors from ten West African and two North African countries; flying over from the home office in Washington to preside over the meeting was the chairman of the board himself, Mr. Sargent Shriver.

The major difference, of course, between the Peace Corps and a large private corporation is that for the former profits have nothing to do with money. A profitable or successful program is one in which the job gets done, whether it involves road surveys in Tanganyika, heavy construction work in Tunisia, medical technology in Togo or teaching in schools throughout most of Africa; it is also one in which administrative and personnel difficulties are lived with, if not actually overcome. The index of success is the request, from the "host country," for more volunteers. By such a standard the Peace Corps is an unqualified, thumping success, for each one of the sixteen countries in Africa, where . . . volunteers . . . are working, has requested more; equally, it is fair to say that, within reasonable limits, "the job is getting done." For an idealistic program, the corps is run on rather practical, hardheaded business lines.

Its problems and frustrations are not very different from those which a large firm encounters when it signs a contract with the government of a new country: administrative skills are scarce, telephone and postal communications are erratic, at best, and disease and problems of health are endemic. But the corps likes

[3] From article in *Economist.* 207:900-1. Je. 1, '63. Reprinted by permission.

to add that its personnel problems are more complicated. For the volunteers are often young, unfamiliar with the country and the situation in which they find themselves and, more to the point, they are untried and untested as men and women. To be blunt, many of them have reached their majority, but not their maturity as yet, and a number of them have been placed in isolated communities, where the loneliness and the break with the habits and needs of their past create obvious psychological pressures. Not surprisingly, then, disaster always lurks around the corner.

One real or imaginary insult to a government . . . and the corps may be threatened with eviction from countries which have only just begun to cease regarding it as neocolonialist. A succession of serious casualties and deaths (there have been six deaths in the field to date) and the staff itself may well decide that the risk is too great, the price too high. . . .

In Nigeria, the physician of the corps has charted the cycles and regions where major diseases occur. Like a traveling salesman, he takes to the road inoculating all the volunteers before the season begins. He spends four fifths of his time in transit and so far there has been no major illness in the corps in Nigeria. He, however, has lost twenty pounds. . . .

Ultimately, the administrators are fond of saying, the program works because of the "kids." They are on their own, they deal with the headmasters and the students, they initiate the community projects, they know the people. In Africa they are usually between twenty-one and twenty-five years of age, though there are three volunteers over fifty and nearly two hundred who fall between the ages of twenty-six and forty.

Two thirds of them are teaching, mostly in secondary schools. Perhaps the most extraordinary thing about "the kids" is precisely how ordinary they are. Relatively few are intellectuals; many come from small towns and rural communities in the Midwest and Far West. They are for the most part unsophisticated and inexperienced; only a small fraction has ever been outside the United States before. It takes them about two months to realize that "what we are doing has little to do with democracy or teach-

ing the American way of life"; and then another two months to
realize that "what we are doing isn't going to change the shape
or destiny of the country." After that one either "calls it quits
and goes home or remains and sticks it out." Since fewer than
twenty-five out of a total of more than five thousand volunteers
have returned home, the reasons for "sticking it out" must be
strong and persuasive.

For some, the chief attraction appears to be a new experience,
slightly exotic, like a strange and peculiar fruit. For others, it is
a challenge, a term of trial, in which they are forced to stretch
their talents, their resources and their character. In the process,
for the young and not so young, the experience seems to provide
an opportunity for exercising responsibility and initiative. Many
take on additional jobs. In Liberia two young teachers have
organized eleven adult education courses in an effort to teach all
the members of their community to read and write. A teacher in
Ghana now devotes part of his holiday to showing the farmers
how to clear the land before planting a new crop, instead of
simply burning all the shrubs away. In Nigeria a handful of
secondary school teachers with American degrees in law is preparing a systematic record of Nigerian case-law. These instances
are more the rule than exceptions to it.

Yet despite the responsibility and the involvement, the volunteers often hint that their view of the real value of the Peace
Corps is rather different from that held in Washington. The concern in Washington for more projects, new countries and a
greater number of volunteers in the field suggests a belief in the
efficacy of the program but it also reflects a desire to increase the
organization's power, making it larger and more important than
it is at present. The volunteers also question the Washington
theory that if they are living an austere life—in a mud hut, with
no air conditioning and a healthy supply of rats scurrying about
the place—then the project must be a success. They contend that
living conditions have little to do with the success or failure of
the corps. And far from having any significant contact with the
adults in the community (another sign of success for Washing-

ton), many of the volunteers have few friends among the local teachers and villagers.

They are willing to grant that the presence of teachers and technicians is valuable to countries all too short of such skilled manpower. As such, they believe that they are making some kind of contribution and "of course it is the justification of the Peace Corps for being." But in the end, they feel, the value to themselves and to the United States will be far greater. They are receiving a practical and most unsentimental education, one which forces them to redefine their assumptions as well as their character. The experience and the knowledge gained, they will tell you, can only serve to strengthen and refurbish their own country. They may very well turn out to be a new breed of voter, a new kind of citizen.

VOLUNTEERS RESENT "HERO" ROLE [4]

The pioneer Peace Corps volunteers are concerned about what they consider an "outlandish image" of themselves being spread among Americans.

They dislike being pictured as heroes, building schools with their bare hands while facing physical hardships in faraway lands.

And they "hate" visitors who take a quick look at a Peace Corps project and say, "You're doing a great job. Keep up the good work."

These are some of the observations developed by the Research Division of the Peace Corps from an intensive study of the first 250 volunteers. The volunteers will complete their two-year tours during June [1963].

Confidential Questionnaire

To get the information, each of the volunteers was required to complete a comprehensive, confidential questionnaire. For the

[4] From "Volunteers Resent 'Hero' Role—Researcher Tells Findings," by David Barnett, North American Newspaper Alliance bureau chief. *Peace Corps Volunteer.* 1:2+. Jl. '63. Reprinted by permission of North American Newspaper Alliance.

past few months, Dr. Joseph G. Colmen, chief of the Research Division, has traveled to units in Tanganyika, Colombia, the Philippines, and St. Lucia, in the West Indies, to hold discussion meetings with the volunteers on the basis of a tabulation of the questionnaire answers.

Dr. Colmen's first reports are now being studied by other Peace Corps divisions—those concerned with selection of volunteers, training, and program development—and may be the basis for changes in the program.

Dr. Colmen, a clinical psychologist, provided a summary of the results so far in an exclusive interview, just before a scheduled trip to Chile to continue the study.

About half the volunteers, he said, experienced some measure of frustration because of a realization that their achievements during the two years did not completely match their personal goals.

Vague Terminology

In some cases, jobs and individuals didn't match.

"Unanticipated things can happen between the time a job is set up and the time a volunteer gets there to fill it," Dr. Colmen explained.

A country, for instance, can ask for a history teacher. When the volunteer gets there, he finds they really need a biology teacher.

"Luckily," he said, "American college students are not so narrowly trained as some think. Many could do it."

In some countries, job descriptions just don't mean the same things that they do in the United States. Terms like "community-development specialist" are nebulous at best. A teacher's aide may turn out to be a person who teaches the teacher what to teach the children.

One of the biggest gripes of the volunteers was about the publicity on the program.

Too often, according to the volunteers, the press—and even the Peace Corps's internal publications—play up the concrete achievements, the road, the schoolhouse, the pigpen, but not the volunteers' efforts of a more subtle but more important nature within the community.

Example: In many underdeveloped areas, the people do not have the drive for success that marks American society. A Peace Corps volunteer organizes the community in a democratic way to get a road built. The important achievement, according to the volunteer, is not the physical road but the fact that the community adopted the approach.

The volunteers also object to the emphasis in the publicity on physical hardship.

"Physical hardship, as such, is no problem," Dr. Colmen pointed out. "The volunteers with the highest morale are those in the most primitive conditions. Given a choice, all of the volunteers would go to the primitive village where it is easiest to see the results of your own efforts."

But there are many of the volunteers in relatively large cities, such as Bogotá. . . .

"These people feel resentful and somewhat guilty at all the publicity about hardship. Friends back home think, 'What's wrong with you? They had to send you to a civilized place.' "

The emphasis, the volunteers contend, should be on the routine, the boredom, the humdrum fighting for maximum effectiveness, not on the glamor aspects of the corps.

"They don't want to be pictured as heroes," Dr. Colmen said, "because they don't think they will be able to live up to the fiction when they get home. And they are convinced the false image will make it more difficult, when they get back, to persuade people to listen to the real facts and problems."

One of the greatest personal problems faced by volunteers overseas is the lack of intellectual stimulation, Dr. Colmen said.

Many of the volunteers are college-trained individuals who are dealing with persons of limited education. From letters and teams of evaluators in the field, the Peace Corps anticipated some of the difficulties that might result from that combination.

To try to help, footlockers of pocket books have been sent to each "household" of volunteers. The footlockers contain a "balanced" collection ranging from the work of Senator Barry Goldwater (Republican of Arizona) to that of President John Kennedy, from history to mystery stories.

Unfortunately, the study of the outgoing volunteers indicates the books did not solve the problem.

"The more you read, the more you want to talk about it," Dr. Colmen said. "Even for volunteers who are in a team operation, discussion with the same person becomes sterile."

Access to Intellectuals?

In some extreme cases, he said, some of the volunteers said that long-term "living with limited sensory stimulation causes them to lose so much of their intellectual drive that they don't even want to read anything."

Some of the volunteers suggested during the study that they need more access to the educated nationals of the host countries.

There is no rule against such mixing, but it does present a conflict situation. The basic idea of the Peace Corps was to get the volunteers out in the field dealing with the grass roots.

Some of the volunteers have met the problem by starting hobbies. Dr. Colmen reported that one, for instance, was making an exhaustive collection of the folk music of Colombia.

As might be expected, some of the volunteers had gripes about Peace Corps administration. Some, the survey showed, feel the Peace Corps did not take care of their needs as quickly as it should have.

These "needs," Dr. Colmen explained, ranged from marital and psychological counseling to such matters as tardy pay checks.

The concern over the tardy pay check, he hastened to point out, was not a personal one: the volunteer was anxious to pay his landlady on time so that the native rooming-house operator would not "lose face."

Dr. Colmen observed that the Peace Corps just did not have enough good supervisors—and could not have—to take care of all these problems, so, in some cases, the volunteer would just have to "sweat it out."

Language Fluency

Most of the volunteers agreed that their effectiveness would be enhanced by greater fluency in the language of the host country.

During training periods, the volunteers are given intensive language training.

"There is a limit to the amount of such training we can give," Dr. Colmen noted. "There are just so many hours of language you can give a student. After that it's wasted time."

The language problem also runs into practical difficulties. To do the most good, the volunteer should have his language facility at the beginning of his tour when he is trying to "break into" the community. After a period, he picks up enough of the language to get along, anyway, so continuation of language training after the volunteers are assigned does not make a big contribution.

Dr. Colmen contended that the gripes about details turned up in the study were an indication that the morale of the volunteers was good.

As he summed it up:

"The volunteers still are deeply committed to the idea and the ideals of the Peace Corps, but they are more realistic about what the Peace Corps can accomplish. And they are more realistic about what it means to be in an organization that, like any other, has administrative problems."

Personal Gain Felt

Many of the 250 volunteers completing service feel that they gained more from the experience than they gave.

The study of the volunteers, made by Dr. Colmen, is full of self-analysis, such as this statement:

"I understand myself better now even though I don't like some of the things I understand. My self as a pre-Peace Corps volunteer is a stranger to my self as a Peace Corps volunteer today."

In general, Dr. Colmen said, the changes in the volunteers as a result of their two-year tours are "healthy." Most consider themselves more mature, more patient, more tolerant, and more self-reliant as a result of their work.

In one of the four country groups studied, 98 per cent of the volunteers reported in their questionnaires that they thought they had made a "contribution" through their Peace Corps work. The lowest percentage reported by any group on the "contribution" question was 65 per cent. Asked if they were "satisfied" with the program, 90 per cent in one group said they were. The lowest group response to the question was 70 per cent.

Of course any bright, youthful American would be expected to mature during two years of work. (The average age of the volunteers is twenty-five.) For research purposes, Dr. Colmen said, the volunteers will be compared with several "control groups."

The "control groups" are college students in the United States and a group of U.S. teachers who have contract jobs—as distinct from volunteers—in East Africa.

Conservative Swing

And, as might be expected, not all of the volunteers changed in the same way.

"One of the perhaps surprising things," Dr. Colmen said, "is that some of the volunteers became more conservative. They think the U.S. should be more reflective in what we do in foreign aid, for instance."

In general, he said, the volunteers are coming out of the program with "much deeper appreciation and pride in America and American standards" although many have questions about what they consider America's materialism, narrowness, and shallowness of interests.

Dr. Colmen said the experience seemed to result in a "confirmation" of the volunteers' belief in social justice. It reinforced their feeling that "personal, material gain is not a truly significant value in life."

As one of the pioneer volunteers put it:

"I have changed somewhat from an extreme idealist to a realist. I recognize the increased importance of honesty and justice. While I appreciate material values, I have a deeper religious faith and greater awareness of the responsibility of being an American."

SOME QUESTIONS AND ANSWERS [5]

MR. [Donald M.] FRASER [Democrat-Farmer-Labor of Minnesota]: Could you tell us some more about the demand . . . [for Peace Corpsmen]?

MR. SHRIVER: With respect to the demand in terms of numbers, we don't have a figure that I would want to put on the record, not because I am hesitant, but because we haven't computed it. There are a number of countries that have asked us for four or five times as many people as are there now. A representative from Thailand was in my office four months ago, who said when the Peace Corps had begun, they were questioning about it, but recently they had a meeting of the cabinet of Thailand and he was authorized to ask us to think in terms of having a thousand volunteers in Thailand alone.

The same thing is true of Pakistan and Nigeria. Two years ago this month that postal card was written in Nigeria and we had thirty-six volunteers then, and most people said that proves that this is a foolish idea, and we better close this business up.

Today we have over four hundred in that country, and two or three weeks ago we had a telephone conversation on that syncom thing, which is a public broadcast as you know, radio, and the minister of education of Nigeria was on that thing and was effusive in his compliments about the Peace Corps and asked us how many more people we could send to Nigeria. He is not the only one. The minister of small business or planning, or whatever they call it over there, is in the same boat. We could easily have one thousand volunteers in Nigeria at their request, not by pushing anything.

[5] From testimony by R. Sargent Shriver, Jr., director of the Peace Corps, before the House of Representatives Committee on Foreign Affairs. In *To Amend the Peace Corps Act;* hearings, October 15-16, 1963, on H.R. 8754. United States. Congress. House of Representatives. Committee on Foreign Affairs. 88th Congress, 1st session. The Committee. Washington, D.C. 20025. '63. p 68-9.

When Haile Selassie was here—we have over four hundred volunteers in Ethiopia—he asked me how soon we could have six hundred over there, and that he wanted as many as he could get, not just in education, but in other areas—agriculture, for example. So the question of—

MR. [H. R.] GROSS [Republican of Iowa]: It helps their balance of payments, doesn't it?

MR. SHRIVER: I don't think it does very much for their balance of payments. We spend very little money over there. For example, in Ethiopia I think the living allowance—I can check it here in a second—the government pays it, the Ethiopian government pays it. They give us $70 a month for every volunteer we have in that country. I might add that Ghana, which has been kicked around here a little bit, pays the full allowance. Liberia also pays part of it.

So it doesn't do their balance of payments an awful lot of good. It does their economic and educational development a lot of good, and they appreciate that. But think of it, Congressman Gross, suppose we knew there were five hundred secondary school teachers in Ethiopia and they all came from Communist Russia and they were teaching all of the school kids in Ethiopia. I think a lot of people in the United States would be worried about that. I would be.

I say the fact that we have almost five hundred schoolteachers in Ethiopia is good. That is the difference.

MR. FRASER: This $70 that you talk about, is that paid—

MR. SHRIVER: By the Ethiopian government.

MR. FRASER: To him?

MR. SHRIVER: To us, the Peace Corps. It is paid through us to the volunteers for their living allowances in that country.

MR. FRASER: That is what I wanted to know.

MR. SHRIVER: That doesn't cover all of it, incidentally. The living allowance in Ethiopia is somewhat more than $70, I believe. All I am trying to indicate is, for a country like Ethiopia, $70 per volunteer is not peanuts.

The other side of the question is we are doing a lot for Ethiopia. We are supplying fine people as teachers in their schools. The fact is they couldn't get their kids into schools if they didn't have them there.

There are a number of schools, not only in Ethiopia but a lot of countries—take Cameroon, where the governor has written us a letter saying if we hadn't been there they would have had to close up half the secondary schools in parts of the country.

Suppose you were President and had to close half the schools. You would be out of office, probably.

MR. FRASER: The limiting factor in filling these additional requests is a lack of availability of the kind of volunteers who are qualified?

MR. SHRIVER: There are three factors. No. 1 is the one you just mentioned—No. 1 is the number of qualified volunteers.

Second is our capacity to manage this thing intelligently and carefully overseas. That is one of the reasons why we are not in seventy-five countries, because we wanted to run it right.

Third was to take it easy until the beneficial results were demonstrable. Now a member of Congress can say to his constituents, "Here are the results, and I think it is worth it from the point of view of the United States." The easiest thing to do—I guess I shouldn't say that, but it seems to be the way to do things frequently—is to get a huge appropriation and find out what to do with the appropriation. As an example, aid to Greece and Turkey. I was here when Congress appropriated $600 million for aid to Greece and Turkey. It went through both Houses in less than six hours.

I found out in the first year they were only able to spend something like $240 million.

We have gone at it the other way. We have said, "Let's justify what we are doing and then we will build on the basis of that." I think the record today fully substantiates that this is in the best interests of the United States, at a minimum cost.

MR. FRASER: I agree with you. Thank you, Mr. Chairman.

CHALLENGE AND RESPONSE [6]

Sargent Shriver reports that on his first trip around the world to discuss the Peace Corps with leaders of potential host countries, more than one voiced the concern of the African leader who told him: "The Peace Corps is a wonderful idea—if only your people could do it." Skepticism concerning America's ability to respond to challenge has come not only from abroad. Many responsible Americans with practical experience in the underdeveloped nations have also expressed doubts.

The reasons for these doubts are many and varied—and in some cases well founded. The personal, economic, environmental, and historic challenges facing each individual volunteer are indeed staggering. And admittedly there has been enough evidence of American "flabbiness" to justify doubts about America's ability to send out pioneers to work on the frontiers of the world. The television documentary "The Flabby American"; Eugene Kinkead's book *In Every War but One,* in which he analyzes the weaknesses of American prisoners of war in Korea; *The Golden Mile* by Herb Elliott, in which the Australian long-distance runner criticizes American youth for their lack of physical stamina; . . . [President Kennedy's] concern over the nation's physical fitness—all reflect widespread concern that softness has become a distinguishing characteristic of our affluent society. "It's a fact," writes Elliott, "that the warm, soft synthetic existence Americans lead poses a real doubt about their future. . . . The fact that Americans have not produced many outstanding distance runners is attributable to their way of life. They are not a hardy race of people; whereas the Norwegians, Russians, and English are."

Doubts about the Peace Corps volunteers' physical stamina, however, are not the only reason for skepticism. "We are sure that there are large numbers of Americans," said the English-language Hong Kong *Tiger Standard,* "who are sincerely eager

[6] From *The Complete Peace Corps Guide* by Roy H. Hoopes, Jr., © 1961 by Roy H. Hoopes, Jr., and reprinted by permission of the publisher, The Dial Press, Inc. New York. '61. p 169-80. Mr. Hoopes is a free-lance writer.

to help the underdeveloped nations. . . . We are not sure, however, how many of these persons will be prepared to have their
living standards reduced to the level of the people among whom
they will be working. Since these people will comprise the
poorer rather than the wealthier portion of the population, this
means that the Peace Corps workers will have to accept a mode
of life not only more uncomfortable than they enjoy at home,
but more uncomfortable also than that enjoyed by the better off
in the country concerned."

Can young Americans be transplanted, with less than four
months' preparation and training, from a soft, overcivilized way
of life to conditions in many cases more rugged than those faced
by American frontiersmen a hundred years ago? . . .

Boredom and physical hardship are not the only challenges.
"The young American idealists," writes commentator Eric
Sevareid about Africa, "are going to be shocked to find a high
percentage of their black counterparts in African colleges totally
inured and indifferent to the suffering of their own countrymen
and interested in freedom, not as individual freedom, but as the
political reshuffle that will give them jobs, big houses, cars and
servants, their true goals in life."

The attitude of the volunteer's counterpart abroad may well
be difficult to cope with—a challenge which has been beautifully
stated by Thomas Loeber in *Foreign Aid, Our Tragic Experiment:*

> On the one hand is the American, a child of centuries of progress
> in Western science and government, who can claim to be the end
> product of the mainstream of civilization and technical innovation. On
> the other hand, we have his foreign counterpart, often the end product
> of thousands of years of stagnation and perhaps centuries of colonialism
> and oppression. Frequently, he may be the first one in the entire history
> of his family who has learned to read or write, or perhaps even to
> wear shoes.
> For at least two years, and usually more (with a break for home
> leave), our American technician must spend more time with this person,
> from day to day and week to week, than he has with anyone else in
> his entire adult life, probably including his own wife.
> They will work long hours together in the office, travel jammed
> together in jeeps for thousands of miles, share the same room, eat out
> of the same dish on occasion, spend days and weeks together in the

field twenty-four hours a day under all kinds of circumstances. And through all this, the American, if he is doing his job, must be friend, teacher, leader, critic, and, above all, student. At the same time, he must, in some way, retain humility, good humor, and dignity. . . the American is on the spot. He is on trial. The burden of proof is on his individual shoulders. He is being judged wherever he goes. He is the makeweight that can tip the scales of a small segment of foreign opinion in the endless balance of the cold war.

In many of the countries to which volunteers will be sent there will be people who are—or at least can quickly become— suspicious of them, if not downright hostile. The average peasant in underdeveloped countries, for instance, is usually suspicious of everyone from the outside and everyone connected with the government, including his own—often with good reason. In addition, in many countries corpsmen will find an infuriating passivity based on the philosophy that extra effort cannot be worth while because man's fate is fixed and determined.

The greatest challenge of all, one which is conceded by every student of international problems, is simply the magnitude of the job that needs to be done. "There is nothing like our villages in America," one representative of the Indian government told a Peace Corps official. "Here it can have up to ten thousand people and still be called a village. The houses are clustered together in a clumsy manner. I wish to utilize the peasant's time in a better way. It takes a month or two for the threshing here. We must find a way to do this more quickly. We have a real struggle with nature. We have to put a great deal in the soil. We have dry land; we have waterlogging. We have the mind and heart to do things, but it takes time to move the people."

There is also the challenge of people themselves—the exploding population. "To travel through the vast areas of the world inhabited by the majority of its people," writes William Vogt in his book *People: Challenge to Survival,* "is to encounter misery so nearly universal and so harrowing as to be almost intolerable to overstuffed Americans who shrink from a challenge to our complacency and optimism." One member of a U.S. agricultural mission in India gave "people" as the main reason he was quitting after only five months on the job. "It's no use," he told the editor of the *Saturday Review;* "you can help one man only to discover fifty men standing behind him. Then you help fifty men and five thousand suddenly appear. You help the five thousand but what do you do about the five million behind them and the fifty million to follow? At some point along the line you decide it's hopeless."

An expert on housing had the same story to tell. "Few nations in human history," he told Norman Cousins, "have made more progress in putting up new housing units than India. Last year, perhaps six to eight millions of people were able to move out of impossibly overcrowded rooms and into decent quarters. But during the same time ten million people were added to the population. The result is that the country is at least two million people worse off than it was a year ago. Can you imagine what the deficit will be ten years from now?"

"Unless population growth can be discouraged," says Eugene Black, president of the International Bank for Reconstruction and Development, "we may have to abandon for this generation our hopes of economic progress in the crowded lands of Asia and the Middle East."

It will be a tremendous challenge for the Peace Corps volunteer to curb his enthusiasm and his urgent desire to see results. One ICA official abroad has estimated that it often takes as long as fifteen years before results of a technical-assistance project can be seen—and even then it is hard to foresee the full impact on the local economy. Aware of this problem, Peace Corps officials have tried to caution volunteers. "Any idealist," wrote Sargent Shriver in *Life,* "must realize that he is not going to change the world overnight. He must realize that he is going to make only a little dent in the problems of underdeveloped areas. His contribution, measured in the whole spectrum of the world's difficulties, will probably cast only a sliver of light—and that sliver may go unseen. After his years of hard work the volunteer may change a few attitudes, but he probably won't be around to see the results. In the Peace Corps the potential for frustration is great."

Then there is the challenge of the cold war. Peace Corps officials are aware of the danger of becoming involved and stress that the Peace Corps is essentially a response to human need: if communism had never come along, two out of every three people in the world would still be living in wretched poverty. As Secretary of State Dean Rusk told the Peace Corps' National Advisory Council, ". . . the Peace Corps is *not* an instrument of foreign policy, because to make it so would rob it of its contribution *to* foreign policy."

It will not be easy to keep out of the cold war. Peace Corps volunteers will have difficulty persuading their hosts that they are not there to stop communism. One young IVS [International Voluntary Services] volunteer wrote home from Vietnam: "In talking to one Vietnamese fellow about American aid, he explained that he is aware that it is only to stop communism before it spread the shooting war to our own soil. . . . He added that if we had really wanted to help just for the sake of helping our fellow men, we would have responded long before the Communist threat."

Obviously, it is up to each individual volunteer abroad, by his conduct and attitude, to convince the people he is working with that he *is* there to help them—not just to stop communism. This challenge will be made all the more difficult by the Russians, who have already labeled the Peace Corps a "crafty plot" and a "Spy Corps"—charges Peace Corps volunteers are likely to hear repeatedly in host countries.

The Communist reaction is understandable. As Walter Lippmann wrote, after an interview with Nikita Khrushchev in April 1961, "there is no doubt that the Soviet government has a relentless determination to foster the revolutionary movement in the underdeveloped countries." One of the reasons most often given for Russia's desire to avoid war is the Soviet belief that time is on the side of the Communists: sooner or later the underdeveloped countries will turn Communist without a shot ever being fired by a Russian soldier. The nature of this conflict was acknowledged by President Kennedy in an address to the nation's newspaper editors on April 20, 1961: "We dare not fail to realize that this struggle is taking place every day, without fanfare, in thousands of villages and markets—day and night—and in classrooms all over the world."

It is not unlikely that Peace Corps volunteers will run into open Communist competition, imitation, or even obstruction. For the present, at least, Russia does not have anything comparable to the Peace Corps. However, experts say the Soviets would have no difficulty finding trained youth to serve abroad if the decision were made to compete with the Peace Corps. Some international Communist youth groups have in fact already been formed. One group built a "Friendship House" in Tunisia; another helped work on the construction of an educational village in Cuba, described in this television newscast over station CKLW, Ontario, Canada (November 15, 1960):

> The project is located in the heart of the country where the Castro revolution sprang up. It is called a school city and young people from forty-five countries are helping to build it up. It will take about five years to complete and will be able to house twenty thousand boys and girls. At the moment, about 180 young men from other parts of the world are supplying the muscle power to raise the buildings. They have been sent there by the World Federation of Democratic Youth—a Communist-organized group. They come from Sweden, Denmark, France, Germany, the Soviet Union, and Eastern countries such as Communist China, North Vietnam, and North Korea. Eight Arab nations are represented. There are not many girls at work, but of the few who did come, one is an American. . . .

Such projects are more in the nature of work-camp operations and are still very few in number. Russia does, however, send out almost as many technical assistants as we do under our Point Four program, and there is good evidence that the Russians are paying more attention now to language training. Foreign languages are compulsory in the elementary and secondary schools, and in some cases Russians have started as early as the age of eight to learn Hindu, Chinese, Urdu, Arabic, and Persian; within five to ten years Russia will have developed an impressive corps of language experts.

Until very recently the Russians have not been much better at mingling with local populations than have Americans abroad.

Russian technicians usually have been no better in coping with local language problems than have Americans. Although they do not live as ostentatiously as many Americans, because they have considerably less money, they are clannish, keeping to themselves, usually in groups of three or four. They have acquired a reputation as fanatic shoppers for consumer goods; whereas the American is considered extravagant, the Russian is considered stingy.

On the other hand, Chinese technical assistants, who are increasing in number every year, always live and mingle with the people of the country in which they are working and have been very successful in establishing contact—especially in Asia. "Our Chinese Communist technicians," a Cambodian official told a *Christian Science Monitor* correspondent, "have simple tastes. They live in wooden barracks. They eat the same food we do. And they work like men possessed—sometimes until eleven at night." State Department experts say this is fairly typical of Chinese Communist technicians in all the countries where they are active (which, in addition to Cambodia, includes Yemen, Nepal, Ceylon, and Guinea).

Wherever Americans are sent, they are going to be the target of Communist activities. There is hardly an underdeveloped area in the world in which a Communist movement is not now active. It will be impossible for Americans serving in any of the underdeveloped countries not to be aware of—or involved in—the struggle going on between two great forces for the minds of men as yet uncommitted to either side. Every time they answer a question about America, every time they do something which makes a lasting impression—for good or bad—on the citizens of the country in which they are working, they will have become involved in the cold war.

It is not surprising that doubts have been raised about America's ability to carry out the objectives of the Peace Corps. Considering the problems involved, it is remarkable how wholeheartedly the youth of America has responded, and how well they have grasped the nature of the task. A new generation seems to be emerging—a generation which often appears in rebellion against the way of life into which it was born; a generation of youth which sees the objectives of the Peace Corps not only as a challenge to America but also as a personal challenge that will prove they are not as soft, silent, and flabby as they have sometimes been made out to be. Many educators have commented on the lack of challenge in ordinary life felt by many young graduates today. "One of our biggest problems is vocational guidance," an educator who is an adviser to the Peace Corps has said. "The young graduates come to us and say: 'How can we get excited about working at a nine-to-five job which we know is of absolutely no significance; about going down to Madison Avenue to help advertising companies sell things people don't need; or about going into law firms which help people who are morally wrong prove they are legally right?'"

This concern over the lack of challenge in our society is not confined to youth. . . . The Peace Corps staff contains numerous professional men who have responded to the urge to serve their country and the challenge of helping the underdeveloped lands. Not untypical is Robert Hellawell, a tax specialist for a Cleveland corporation law firm, who feels everyone should spend at least part of his career in public service. Hellawell is now the Peace Corps representative in Tanganyika.

However, in responding to this challenge, the younger generation wants to do it their way—which is not necessarily the way America has been doing it. Dean Bowman, for instance, a twenty-six-year-old veteran of two years in Laos as an IVS volunteer, gave some indication of what the younger generation is thinking when he addressed a group of college presidents, businessmen, and labor leaders assembled last year to discuss the pros and cons of the Peace Corps: "I am not trying to slam your generation," he said, "but I don't think that young people are very much challenged by the way in which America's role in the world has been presented in the past. It has been presented in terms of massive retaliation, in essentially negative terms. I know that this personally does not fire my imagination, or that of my contemporaries. They don't mind going into the boondocks—the rural areas—and they have the vitality to eat the bad food and have the stomach upsets and yet still make a human impact. This idea, of positively applying America's know-how and moral power, does fire our imagination—tremendously. This, to young people, is a very significant challenge."

Others have noted the same stirrings: the *Saturday Review,* for instance, said, "The big news today is that the slumber party is over. The college campus has come fully alive. The reason for it goes by the name of the American Peace Corps. . . . Instead of dreary conversations about the meaninglessness of existence, students are now earnestly exchanging ideas about the different needs of communities in Asia and Africa. They are matching their abilities to the problems of the underdeveloped nations. . . . Idealism is back in style." . . .

There can be little doubt that the nation's youth has been taken with the idea of serving abroad in an "army of peace"— and with much more enthusiasm than William James ever dreamed of. Every day another newspaper story or magazine article or an essay in a student journal quotes another young American's desire to serve. It is expressed especially well by a young man named George Albert Johnson, chosen by his group— a contingent of Peace Corps volunteers in training at Texas Western—to talk to the other students of the college. "I think we have chosen to join the Peace Corps," said Johnson, "for a relatively simple reason—we couldn't, in all conscience, follow any other course; each of us is convinced that America is a strong country, a great country. Each of us realizes its strength and greatness and wide responsibility, a responsibility to less fortunate nations. We don't want them to feel economically indebted to America—we want them to feel that America's strength and wealth is best realized by the amount of help we are able to offer. All of us have been interested in the Peace Corps since its inception, and we believe in the ideal of responsibility that it represents. Believing as we do in America's responsibilities as a nation and in our responsibilities as a citizen of that nation, we have chosen to match our actions with our convictions in serving the Peace Corps. We feel it is an honor to be chosen to serve.

Each of us is humbled by the fact that out of thousands, we were the ones to be selected. During our service with the Peace Corps, we are going to try our best to deserve the honor of representing America to the nations of the world. We submit that we are not dewy-eyed young zealots, as some people have called us, out to save the world, but instead reasonably mature citizens with a skill to offer others and a sincere conviction that the Peace Corps can be a contributing part of America's leadership to the underdeveloped nations of the world."

THE PEACE CORPS' STRENGTH [7]

In the beginning, the doubters worried about the callowness of youth and the ability of mortals to make any good idea work. The more recent criticism is more sophisticated and more substantive. Eric Sevareid recently observed:

While the corps has something to do with spot benefits in a few isolated places, whether in sanitizing drinking water or building culverts, its work has, and can have, very little to do with the fundamental investments, reorganizations and reforms upon which the true and long-term economic development of backward countries depends.

Mr. Sevareid acknowledges that "giving frustrated American youth a sense of mission and adding to our supply of comprehension of other societies fatten the credit side of the ledger." He adds: "If fringe benefits were all the corps' originators had in mind, then this should be made clear to the country." I do not agree with him that the second and third purposes of the Peace Corps Act—representing America abroad in the best sense and giving Americans an opportunity to learn about other societies— are "fringe benefits." [The first objective of the Peace Corps is to make skilled manpower available to interested nations.—Ed.] Fulton Freeman, the United States ambassador in Colombia [appointed ambassador to Mexico in 1964], believes the whole Peace Corps program could be justified by its creation of a new

[7] From "Two Years of the Peace Corps," by R. Sargent Shriver, Jr., director of the Peace Corps. Excerpted by special permission from *Foreign Affairs*, 41:703-7. July 1963. Copyright by the Council on Foreign Relations Inc., New York.

American resource in the volunteers who are acquiring language skills and intensive understanding of a foreign society. Former volunteers will be entering government service (150 have already applied to join USIA [United States Information Agency]), United Nations agencies, academic life, international business concerns and a host of other institutions which carry on the business of the United States throughout the world. Others will return to their homes, capable of exerting an enlightened influence in the communities where they settle. Many trite euphemisms of the ignorant and ready panaceas of the uninformed will clash immediately with the harsh facts that volunteers have learned to live with abroad.

Is the second purpose of the Peace Corps Act—to be a good representative of our society—a "fringe benefit"? Peace Corps volunteers are reaching the people of foreign countries on an individual basis at a different level from the influence of most Americans abroad. The Peace Corps volunteer lives under local laws, buys his supplies at local stores and makes his friends among local people. He leaves to the diplomat and the technicians the complex tools which are peculiarly their own while he sets out to work in the local environment as he finds it.

I am not suggesting that life for the volunteer is always hard. A visiting Ghanaian said: "The Peace Corps teachers in my country don't live so badly. After all, they live as well as we do." I agree that this is not so bad; nor is our objective discomfort for discomfort's sake, but rather a willingness to share the life of another people, to accept sacrifice when sacrifice is necessary and to show that material privilege has not become the central and indispensable ingredient in an American's life. It is interesting to note that the happiest volunteers are usually those with the most difficult living conditions.

Although I disagree with Mr. Sevareid's emphasis in dismissing two of the three purposes of the Peace Corps Act as "fringe benefits," he does get to the heart of an important question when he compares the direct economic impact of the Peace Corps to fundamental investments, reorganizations and economic development. The Peace Corps' contribution has been less in direct economic development than in social development—health, education, construction and community organization. We are convinced that economic development directly depends on social development. In his valedictory report this past April as head of the [United Nations] Economic Commission for Latin America, Raúl Prebisch observed that there are *not*

grounds for expecting that economic development will take place first and be followed in the natural course of events by social development. Both social and economic development must be achieved in measures that require the exercise of rational and deliberate action. . . . There can be no speed-up in economic development without a change in the social structure.

While they have their differences, Theodore W. Schultz and J. Kenneth Galbraith [noted economists] have no disagreement on the essential role of social development in economic progress. In contrast, some who argue from the European-North American experience overlook the vital need for social development which had already been substantially achieved in the countries of the Atlantic community. This is the basic difference between the problem of the Marshall Plan, which was concerned with economic reconstruction in societies with abundant social resources, and the problem of forced-draft economic development in much of Asia, Africa and Latin America.

Notwithstanding the Peace Corps' primary emphasis on social development, volunteers are making a direct economic contribution in a variety of situations. They are helping to organize farmers' cooperatives in Chile, Ecuador and Pakistan; credit unions and savings and loan associations in Latin America; demonstration farms in the Near East. A group of volunteers in the Punjab sparked the creation of a poultry industry of some economic significance (using ground termite mounds for protein feed). These are grass-roots projects. More of them will someday cause us to look back and wonder why it took so long to discover that people—human hands and enthusiasms—are an essential part of the relationship of mutual assistance which we must establish with our neighbors abroad.

The Peace Corps is not a "foreign aid" agency. Two of the three purposes of the Peace Corps as defined in the Act deal with understanding, not economic assistance. Moreover, our financial investment is in the volunteer who brings his skills and knowledge home with him. Seventy-five per cent of the Peace Corps' appropriated funds enters the economy of the United States; of the remaining 25 per cent, more than half (57 per cent) is spent on American citizens, the Peace Corps volunteers themselves.

A Jamaican radio commentator recently asserted that "a great distance between people is the best creator of good will. Jumble people up together on a sort of temporary basis of gratitude on one side and condescension on the other, and you'll have everyone at each other's throat in no time." If I believed this were inevitable, regardless of the attitude, preparation and mode of life of volunteers, I would advocate disbanding the Peace Corps—as well as most other programs overseas. But I have greater faith in the universality of men's aspirations and of men's ability to respect each other when they know each other. It is the American who lives abroad in isolation and the thoughtless tourist who create distrust and dislike.

I believe the Peace Corps is also having more impact than we may realize on our own society and among our own people. To take an example of the Peace Corps' impact on an institution, the president of the State University of Iowa, Virgil M. Hancher, recently observed:

> The Peace Corps project (training volunteers for Indonesia) is already having salutary effects upon this university, and these seem likely to be residual. The members of our faculty are having to come together across disciplines. They are having to think through old problems of education freshly and to tackle new ones. Along with the trainees, they are learning—learning how to teach languages in the new method, how to teach new languages, how to teach area studies better, and how to adapt old and test new methods. The project is deepening the international dimension of the State University of Iowa. This international dimension is being shared, in various ways, with the people of the state, the eastern area in particular.

American schools and students may soon benefit from the Peace Corps' initiative in another fashion. Two countries, Ghana and Argentina, have expressed interest in making the Peace Corps a two-way street by sending volunteer teachers of special competence to interested American high schools or colleges. Ghana would provide experts in African history and Argentina teachers of Spanish. Other countries may follow suit.

Our own Peace Corps volunteers are being changed in other ways in the acquisition of languages and expertise. They will be coming home more mature, with a new outlook toward life and work. Like many other Americans, I have wondered whether our contemporary society, with its emphasis on the organizational man and the easy life, can continue to produce the self-reliance, initiative and independence that we consider to be part of our heritage. We have been in danger of losing ourselves among the motorized toothbrushes, tranquilizers and television commercials. Will Durant [historian and author] once observed that nations are born stoic and die epicurean; we have been in danger of this happening to us. The Peace Corps is truly a new frontier in the sense that it provides the challenge to self-reliance and independent action which the vanished frontier once provided on our own continent. Sharing in the progress of other countries helps us to rediscover ourselves at home.

The influence of the Peace Corps idea might be described as a series of widening circles, like the expanding rings from a stone thrown into a pond. The inner, most sharply defined circle represents the immediate effect of the program—accomplishments abroad in social and economic development, skills, knowledge, understanding, institution-building, a framework for cooperative effort with private organizations, research and experiment in "overseas Americanship," language training and improvements in health.

The second ring moving outward on the water might be the Peace Corps' influence on our society, on institutions and people, on the creation of a new sense of participation in world events, an influence on the national sense of purpose, self-reliance and an expanded concept of volunteer service in time of peace.

There is still a wider circle and, being farthest from the splash, the hardest to make out clearly. Perhaps I can explain it by describing the relationships I see between the Peace Corps and our American Revolution. The Revolution placed on our citizens the responsibility for reordering their own social structure. It was a triumph over the idea that man is incompetent or incapable of shaping his destiny. It was our declaration of the irresistible strength of a universal idea connected with human dignity, hope, compassion and freedom. The idea was not simply American, of course, but arose from a confluence of history, geography and the genius of a resolute few at Philadelphia.

We still have our vision, but our society has been drifting away from the world's majority: the young and raw, the colored, the hungry and the oppressed. The Peace Corps is helping to put us again where we belong. It is our newest hope for rejoining the majority of the world without at the same time betraying our cultural, historic, political and spiritual ancestors and allies. As Pablo Casals, the renowned cellist and democrat, said of the Peace Corps last year: "This is new, and it is also very old. We have come from the tyranny of the enormous, awesome, discordant machine back to a realization that the beginning and the end are man—that it is man who is important, not the machine, and that it is man who accounts for growth, not just dollars and factories. Above all, that it is man who is the object of all our efforts."

BIBLIOGRAPHY

An asterisk (*) preceding a reference indicates that the article or a part of it has been reprinted in this book.

BOOKS, PAMPHLETS, AND DOCUMENTS

Albertson, M. L. and others. New frontiers for American youth; perspective on the Peace Corps. Public Affairs Press. Washington, D.C. 20002. '61.

Foreign Policy Association. World Affairs Center. Careers in world affairs; at home and abroad. Doubleday. Garden City, N.Y. '61.

*Hayes, S. P. International Peace Corps, the promise and problems. Public Affairs Institute. Washington, D.C. 20002. '61.
   Reprinted in this book: Central purpose. p 8-10; Earlier proposals and other programs. p 14-19.

*Hoopes, Roy H., Jr. Complete Peace Corps guide. Dial Press. New York. '61.

Horowitz, A. H. Outlook for youth. (Reference Shelf v 34, no 1) Wilson. New York. '62.

International Conference on Middle Level Manpower. Hidden force: a report of the conference. Harper. New York. '63.

*James, William. Memories and studies. Longmans. New York. '11.
   Reprinted in this book: Moral equivalent of war. p 267:96.

Loeber, T. S. Foreign aid: our tragic experiment. Norton. New York. '61.

Obi, Enuenwemba. Peace-corpsism. Pageant Press. New York. '62.

*Rockefeller, David. Managerial work and human progress; address before 13th International Management Congress of Comité International de l'Organisation Scientifique, New York, September 16-20, 1963. Council for International Progress in Management (USA), Inc. 247 Park Ave., New York 10017. '63.

Rollman, H. W. World construction. Greenberg. New York. '54.

*United States. Congress. House of Representatives. Our nation's youth; message to Congress, February 14, 1963. J. F. Kennedy. (H. Doc. no 66) 88th Congress, 1st session. Supt. of Docs. Washington, D.C. 20025. '63.

*United States. Congress. House of Representatives. Permanent Peace Corps; message to Congress, March 1, 1961. J. F. Kennedy. (H. Doc. no 98) 87th Congress, 1st session. Supt. of Docs. Washington, D.C. 20025. '61.

  Same: Vital Speeches of the Day. 27:325-7. Mr. 15, '61.

*United States. Congress. House of Representatives. Committee on Foreign Affairs. To amend the Peace Corps Act; hearings, October 15-16, 1963, on H.R. 8754. 88th Congress, 1st session. The Committee. Washington, D.C. 20025. '63.

  Reprinted in this book: Statement. R. S. Shriver, Jr. p3-8; Peace Corps-CARE: experiment in community development. Fulton Freeman. p 60-7; Testimony. R. S. Shriver, Jr. p 68-9.

United States. International Cooperation Administration. Peace Corps: final report; a study by Colorado State University Research Foundation, Fort Collins, Colorado. M. L. Albertson and A. E. Rice. The Administration. Washington, D.C. 20025. '61.

*United States. Peace Corps. Peace Corps; 2nd annual report. The corps. Washington, D.C. 20525. '63.

  Reprinted in this book: Operations. p 34-9.

United States. Peace Corps. Peace Corps fact book. The corps. Washington, D.C. 20525. '61.

*Wells, H. G. New world order. Secker and Warburg. New York. '40.

  Reprinted in this book: World Order in Being. p 161-91.

*Wingenbach, C. E. Peace Corps—who, how, and where. John Day. New York. '61.

  Reprinted in this book: Peace Corps training in action. p 78-85.

PERIODICALS

America. 104:746. Mr. 11, '61. Peace Corps shapes up.

America. 104:776. Mr. 18 '61. Accent on youth. Mary McGrory.

America. 104:789-90. Mr. 18, '61. Catholic campuses view the Peace Corps plan. F. P. Canavan.

America. 104:808. Mr. 24, '61. Peace Corps requirements. Howard Penniman.

America. 105:49-50. Ap. 8, '61. No children's crusade; summary of interviews; African and Asian personnel at the UN.

America. 105:72-3. Ap. 8, '61. Paying the price for peace. R. M. Barlow.

America. 105:274-5. My. 13, '61. How we look to others. C. J. McNaspy.

America. 105:706-7. S. 9, '61. Open letter to Newman clubs. T. E. Quigley.

America. 106:16-18. O. 7, '61. Peace Corps revisited. R. M. Barlow.

America. 106:318. D. 2, '61. Peace Corps report; inspection tour of Latin America.

America. 106:809. Mr. 24, '62. Healthy yearling.

America. 107:4. Ap. 7, '62. Youth in perspective.

America. 107:453. Jl. 7, '62. Youth's potential.

America. 107:459-61. Jl. 7, '62. Friends in Washington. N. K. Herzfeld.

America. 107:1167. D. 1, '62. Peace Corps and the churches.

America. 108:69, 71+. Ja. 19, '63. Who is joining the Peace Corps? Disturbing questions about Catholic participation; with editorial comment. J. M. Cronin and T. E. Cronin.

American Society of Civil Engineers Proceedings. 89 [SU 2 no 3536]: 13-25. Je. '63. First Peace Corps surveyors and engineers. R. C. Brinker.

Américas. 15:2-10. Jl. '63. Volunteers for progress; Peace Corps in Latin America. N. A. Haverstock.

Bulletin of the Atomic Scientists. 17:160-1. Ap. '61. New Peace Corps.

Business Week. p 144. Mr. 11, '61. What the Peace Corps can do; U.S. public relations weapon.

*Chemical and Engineering News. 41:92-4. F. 18, '63. Peace Corps couple typify new trend.

Christian Century. 78:317. Mr. 15, '61. Not for propaganda but for peace.
> Discussion: 78:563. My. 3. '61.

Christian Century. 78:450-2. Ap. 12, '61. Peace Corps in perspective; questions and answers. C. F. Stoerker.

Christian Century. 79:101. Ja. 24, '62. Peace Corps problems akin to those of missions.

Christian Century. 79:1380-2. N. 14, '62. Church view of the Peace Corps. C. F. Stoerker.

Christian Century. 80:701. My. 29, '63. Hundreds of senior citizens wanted.

*Commonweal. 72:146-8. My. 6, '60. Point Four youth corps. H. S. Reuss.

Commonweal. 73:377. Ja. 6, '61. Peace Corps plan.

Commonweal. 73:625. Mr. 17, '61. Peace Corps plan; pilot model.

Commonweal. 74:198. My. 19, '61. Daughters of the American what? James O'Gara.

Commonweal. 75:142. N. 3, '61. Innocence abroad. James O'Gara.

Congressional Digest. 39:295-313. D. '60. Proposed Federal Youth Conservation Corps; with pro and con discussion.

*Department of State Bulletin. 44:551-2. Ap. 17, '61. Internationalizing the concept of the Peace Corps; address, March 28, 1961. Harlan Cleveland.

Department of State Bulletin. 44:583. Ap. 24, '61. President Kennedy names members of Peace Corps Advisory Council.

Department of State Bulletin. 44:1005-6. Je. 26, '61. Plan for international development; statement, June 7, 1961. Dean Rusk.

Department of State Bulletin. 45:603. O. 9, '61. Peace Corps legislation signed into law by President Kennedy; statement, September 22, 1961. J. F. Kennedy.

Department of State Bulletin. 46:521. Mr. 26, '62. President recommends expansion of the Peace Corps; text of letter, February 26, 1962. J. F. Kennedy.

Department of State Bulletin. 47:329-30. Ag. 27, '62. President issues executive order on the administration of the Peace Corps. J. F. Kennedy.

Department of State Bulletin. 47:333-8. Ag. 27, '62. America's interest in African education. J. W. Fredericks.

Department of State Bulletin. 47:853-9. D. 3, '62. Human skills in the decade of development; summary report. International Conference on Middle Level Manpower, San Juan, Puerto Rico.

*Department of State Bulletin. 49:170-2. Jl. 29, '63. President recommends expansion of Peace Corps; letter to Lyndon B. Johnson and John W. McCormack, July 4, 1963. J. F. Kennedy.

Department of State Bulletin. 49:198-9. Ag. 5, '63. President Nyerere of Tanganyika visits Washington; joint communique, July 16, 1963; with announcement of new Peace Corps agreement. M. J. K. Nyerere and J. F. Kennedy.

Department of State Bulletin. 50:198. F. 10, '64. President requests increased appropriation for Peace Corps. L. B. Johnson.

Ebony. 17:38-40+. N. '61. Peace Corps; Negroes play vital role.

Ebony. 18:69-70+. N. '62. Peace Corps training at Howard.

*Economist. 202:909. Mr. 10, '62. Peace Corps; happy birthday.

*Economist. 207:900-1. Je. 1, '63. Unsentimental journey.

Editorial Research Reports. 1:3-20. Ja. 4, '61. Government youth corps. H. B. Shaffer.

Editorial Research Reports. 2:855-72. N. 28, '62. Peace Corps expansion. H. B. Shaffer.

*Editorial Research Reports. 1:249-64. Ap. 3, '63. Domestic Peace Corps. H. B. Shaffer.

*Foreign Affairs. 41:694-707. Jl. '63. Two years of the Peace Corps. R. S. Shriver, Jr.

Foreign Policy Bulletin. 40:68-70. Ja. 15, '61. Would a Peace Corps be useful? Foreign Policy forum. Michael Belshaw; Franklin Wallick.

Good Housekeeping. 156:84-5+. Ap. '63. My life as a Peace Corps girl; ed. by Andrew St. George. J. C. Boegli.

*Harper's Magazine. 223:63-8. S. '61. Peace Corps' secret mission. Benjamin DeMott.

Human Organization. 21:286-9. Wint. '62-'63. Tanganyika and the Peace Corps: unanswered questions. Scott Gilbert.

Library Journal. 88:4448. N. 15, '63. Peace Corps needs 9,000 in 1964.

Life. 50:34-41. Mr. 17, '61. Peace Corps catches fire in colleges; with account by R. S. Shriver, Jr.

Life. 51:84. O. 27, '61. Much ado about a postcard.

Look. 25:34-7. N. 7, '61. On trial, Sargent Shriver and the Peace Corps.

Mademoiselle. 53:276+. Ag. '61. Cautious crusaders. M. A. Guitar.

Mademoiselle. 57:126-9+. Je. '63. Doers, not do-gooders, the Peace Corps in Nigeria. H. L. Callaway.

Mechanical Engineering. 84:96-8. D. '62. Peace Corps engineers on technical training jobs around the world.

NEA Journal. 50:26. My. '61. What teachers should know about the Peace Corps.

NEA Journal. 51:48-9. Ap. '62. Mango for the Peace Corps teacher. R. S. Shriver, Jr.

NEA Journal. 52:13-14+. Mr. '63. When Peace Corps teachers return. R. S. Shriver, Jr.

Nation. 191:430-2. D. 3, '60. New frontier: the Peace Corps; Princeton conference. A. C. Elms.

Nation. 192:225. Mr. 18, '61. Peace Corps.

National Review. 10:171-2. Mr. 25, '61. Ah yes, the Peace Corps.

National Review. 10:188. Mr. 25, '61. What about the Peace Corps? David Franke.

National Review. 10:211-12. Ap. 8, '61. Peace, it's wonderful. A. L. Moats.

National Review. 11:195. S. 25, '61. Peace Corps in reverse? D. N. Rowe.

National Review. 12:356. My. 22, '62. Discorps.

Negro History Bulletin. 25:32. N. '61. Madge Shipp and the Peace Corps. Mildred Pitt.

New Republic. 144:3-4. Mr. 13, '61. Peace Corps.

New Republic. 144:9. Mr. 20, '61. Peace Corps at home.

New Republic. 144:4-5. Je. 12, '61. Peace Corps is born.

New Republic. 145:4-5. O. 30, '61. Borrioboola-Gha.

New Republic. 145:8-9. N. 6, '61. Question of black or white. Paul Conklin.

*New York Times. p 32. N. 3, '60. Excerpts from Kennedy's speech urging U.S. "Peace Corps." J. F. Kennedy.

New York Times. p E5. Ja. 14, '62. Peace Corps finds it is in demand. Peter Braestrup.

New York Times. p 8. Mr. 6, '63. Shriver's Peace Corps and the New Frontier. James Reston.

New York Times. p 10. Ag. 17, '63. Peace Corps women complain that the living is easy. Rita Reif.

New York Times. p 3. S. 5, '63. Indians in Andes advance from peonage. Juan de Onís.

New York Times. p 72. Ja. 20, '64. Peace Corps rides a goodwill road. R. B. Semple, Jr.

New York Times. p 1+. F. 2, '64. Shriver is chosen to head campaign against poverty. J. D. Morris.

New York Times. p 48. F. 9, '64. Union "Peace Corps" aids Latin nations.

New York Times Magazine. p 26+. F. 5, '61. Force of youth as a force for peace. Gertrude Samuels.

New York Times Magazine. p 9+. My. 14, '61. Challenges to the Peace Corps. G. H. T. Kimble.

New York Times Magazine. p 11+. D. 17, '61. Peace Corpsman no. 1, a progress report. Peter Braestrup.

New York Times Magazine. p 106+. O. 14, '62. Old volunteers? R. S. Shriver, Jr.

New York Times Magazine. p 36-7. O. 21, '62. Peace Corps trains in New York. Gertrude Samuels.

*New York Times Magazine. p 34+. N. 25, '62. Peace Corps for our own bleak areas. Gertrude Samuels.

New York Times Magazine. p 34+. Je. 9, '63. I have the best job in Washington. R. S. Shriver, Jr.

*New Yorker. 38:24-7. Je. 30, '62. Pioneers.

New Yorker. 39:50-2+. S. 28, '63. Reporter at large; Peace Corps in the Philippines. Robert Shaplen.

Newsweek. 57:19-20. Mr. 13, '61. Answering the call.

Newsweek. 57:30. Mr. 20, '61. Peace Corps. E. K. Lindley.

Newsweek. 57:31-2. Ap. 17, '61. Peace Corps: outward bound.

Newsweek. 57:35-6. My. 1, '61. Tanganyika ho.

Newsweek. 57:23-4. My. 22, '61. Clicks and thumps.

Newsweek. 57:36. Je. 12, '61. We were pooped; qualifying tests.

Newsweek. 58:43. Jl. 10, '61. Better way.

Newsweek. 58:20. S. 4, '61. Eye of the storm.

Newsweek. 58:28+. O. 30, '61. Story of a postcard.

Newsweek. 58:13-16. D. 25, '61. Peace Corps on Christmas Eve.
    Same abridged with title: Peace Corps one year later. Reader's Digest. 80:
    146-9: Mr. '62.

Newsweek. 60:47-8. O. 22, '62. More Peace Corps.

*Newsweek. 61:48. Je. 3, '63. Colombia; Señor Ron; with report by
    M. J. Kubic.

Occupational Outlook Quarterly. 5:11-15. S. '61. Opportunities for
    service in the Peace Corps. R. S. Bryan.

Parents' Magazine & Better Homemaking. 38:46-7+. Jl. '63. Peace
    Corps; frontier for youth. R. S. Shriver, Jr.

*Peace Corps Volunteer. 1:2+. Jl. '63. Volunteers resent "hero" role—
    researcher tells findings. David Barnett.

Peace Corps Volunteer. 1:10-13. Jl. '63. Peru. D. S. Palmer.

Peace Corps Volunteer. 1:13-14. Jl. '63. 20th century is dawning in the
    Andes. Paul Doughty.

Peace Corps Volunteer. 1:22-3. Jl. '63. Additional career opportunities
    for volunteers who are completing two years of service.

Peace Corps Volunteer. 1:6-8. S. '63. Turkey. D. N. Weinman.

Peace Corps Volunteer. 1:16-18. S. '63. Dominican Republic. Andres
    Hernandez.

Peace Corps Volunteer. 1:2-3. O. '63. Here's how they see it now.

Peace Corps Volunteer. 1:8. O. '63. Returning volunteers urged to be
    active in educating Americans on foreign relations. S. P. Hayes.

Peace Corps Volunteer. 2:6-7+. N. '63. "Vacation" is teachers' plight.
    Ginna Frank.

Peace Corps Volunteer. 2:10-11. N. '63. Jamaica: "No place like home!"
    Carol Schnebel.

Peace Corps Volunteer. 2:12-13. N. '63. Nyasaland; a free land in
    1964: Malawi.

*Peace Corps Volunteer. 2:6-8. F. '64. "You just plunge in." M. M.
    McEvoy.

*Progressive. 26:19-22. Ag. '62. Peace Corps wins its way. T. W.
    Ottenad.

Recreation. 55:233-4. My. '62. Recreation in the Peace Corps.

Recreation. 56:356-8. O. '63. Broad horizons. Ruth Schumm.

Reporter. 26:35-6. F. 1, '62. Peace Corps comes to Tanganyika. J. P. Nugent.

Saturday Evening Post. 235:77-81. S. 8, '62. Profile of a Peace Corpsman; George Kroon. N. A. Haverstock.

Saturday Evening Post. 236:78-81. My. 4, '63. Ugly American revisited. Eugene Burdick and W. J. Lederer.

Saturday Review. 43:28. D. 24, '60. Is a national Peace Corps enough? Youth cadres for peace. George Fersh.

Saturday Review. 44:17-19+. Je. 17, '61. Can the Peace Corps do the job? G. E. Sokolsky; R. S. Shriver, Jr.
    Discussion: 44:27. Jl. 8, '61.

Saturday Review. 46:42-4+. Jl. 20, '63. Teachers in the Peace Corps. Mike Edwards.

School and Society. 89:135. Mr. 25, '61. Peace Corps and educational competence. W. W. Brickman.

School Life. 45:27. Ap. '63. Forty-four countries call.

Science. 133:977. Mr. 31, '61. Idealism for export. Graham DuShane.

Science News Letter. 79:323. My. 27, '61. Volunteers safeguarded.

Science News Letter. 83:165. Mr. 16, '63. PCV an American image. Watson Davis.

Senior Scholastic. 78:40-1+. F. 8, '61. Youth for Peace Corps? Daniel Chu.

Senior Scholastic. 78:18. Mr. 15, '61. Reveille for the Peace Corps.

Senior Scholastic. 78:11-12. My. 3, '61. Teens sound off on foreign aid.

Senior Scholastic. 79:14-16+. S. 27, '61. Peace Corps: ready, set, go! W. P. Lineberry.

Senior Scholastic. 79:30+. N. 1, '61. Card that strayed.

Senior Scholastic. 80:16. Mr. 14, '62. Help wanted!

Senior Scholastic. 82:6-9. Mr. 13, '63. Peace Corps after two years.

Senior Scholastic. 82:1T+. Ap. 17, '63. Teachers wanted.

Seventeen. 20:20+. Jl. '61. Peace Corps; questions and answers.

Seventeen. 21:174+. My. '62. If you hope to join the Peace Corps. R. H. Hoopes, Jr.

Seventeen. 22:152-3+. My. '63. Inside the Peace Corps.

Sports Illustrated. 17:28-30+. D. 10, '62. Wanted; thirty-two guys for the boondocks; volunteers to coach in Indonesia. Gilbert Rogin.

Successful Farming. 59:17. Jl. '61. Peace Corps needs farm men and women; interview. R. S. Shriver, Jr.

Successful Farming. 59:22. Ag. '61. Across the editor's desk. Dick Hanson.

Time. 77:59. F. 24, '61. Go everywhere, young man.

Time. 77:18+. Mr. 10, '61. Newest frontier.

Time. 77:24-5. Ap. 7, '61. How about Urdu?

Time. 77:12-13. My. 12, '61. Peace Corpsman.

Time. 78:30-1. Ag. 11, '61. Peace Corps boot camps.

Time. 78:22-3. S. 8, '61. And away they go!

Time. 78:24. O. 27, '61. She had no idea.

Time. 78:20-1. N. 17, '61. Corpsmen in Ghana.

Time. 78:10-11. D. 29, '61. Report on the Peace Corps.

Time. 80:35-6. Jl. 13, '62. West at its best.

Time. 82:18-22. Jl. 5, '63. It is almost as good as its intentions.

U.S. News & World Report. 50:44-5. Mr. 13, '61. ABC of Kennedy's Peace Corps.

U.S. News & World Report. 50:58. Mr. 20, '61. Peace Corps: old story to U.S. missionaries.

U.S. News & World Report. 50:90. Ap. 3, '61. Peace Corps: its director tells what to expect; excerpts from hearing before the Senate Foreign Relations Committee. R. S. Shriver, Jr.

U.S. News & World Report. 51:40-2. Jl. 24, '61. Truth about the Peace Corps.

U.S. News & World Report. 51:4. O. 30, '61. Peace Corps suffers some growing pains.

U.S. News & World Report. 51:68-70. D. 4, '61. On the job with the Peace Corps in Africa and South America.

U.S. News & World Report. 53:15. O. 22, '62. Copying the Peace Corps.

U.S. News & World Report. 53:72-5. D. 10, '62. Close-up of the Peace Corps one year later; Zipacon, Colombia. C. B. Richardson.

U.S. News & World Report. 54:16. Ja. 7, '63. High office for another JFK kinsman?

Vital Speeches of the Day. 27:395-7. Ap. 15, '61. Peace Corps idea; address, March 22, 1961. H. O. Staggers.

*Vital Speeches of the Day. 28:407-11. Ap. 15, '62. Job was tough; address before 17th National Conference on Higher Education, Chicago, March 6, 1962. R. S. Shriver, Jr.

Vogue. 141:91. F. 1, '63. Vogue's eye view of a loving sign.

*Wilson Library Bulletin. 36:833-4. Je. '62. Librarian in the Peace Corps. Jean Ellickson.